ASTRONOMICAL!

An awesome encounter with the wonders of the universe

DK

Smithsonian

Senior Editor Shaila Brown
Senior Art Editor Smiljka Surla
Editors Jolyon Goddard, Ben Morgan
US Editor Jill Hamilton
US Executive Editor Lori Cates Hand
Designer Rhys Thomas
Illustrators Peter Bull Art Studio,
Diarmuid Ó Caitháin/NB Illustration
Managing Editor Rachel Fox
Managing Art Editor Owen Peyton Jones
Production Editor Dragana Puvacic
Production Controller Joss Moore
Jacket Designers Smiljka Surla, Surabhi Wadhwa
Picture Researchers Sumedra Chopra, Manpreet Kaur, Jo Walton
Art Director Mabel Chan
Publisher Andrew Macintyre

Authors Sophie Allan, Josh Barker, Isabel Thomas
Consultant Professor Katherine Blundell OBE, University of Oxford

First American Edition, 2025
Published in the United States by DK Publishing,
a division of Penguin Random House LLC
1745 Broadway, 20th Floor, New York, NY 10019

Copyright © 2025 Dorling Kindersley Limited
25 26 27 28 29 10 9 8 7 6 5 4 3 2 1
001–342552–Apr/2025

All rights reserved.
Without limiting the rights under the copyright reserved above, no part of this publication may be reproduced, stored in or introduced into a retrieval system, or transmitted, in any form, or by any means (electronic, mechanical, photocopying, recording, or otherwise), without the prior written permission of the copyright owner.
Published in Great Britain by Dorling Kindersley Limited

A catalog record for this book
is available from the Library of Congress.
ISBN 978-0-5939-6454-5

DK books are available at special discounts when purchased in bulk for sales promotions, premiums, fund-raising, or educational use.
For details, contact: DK Publishing Special Markets,
1745 Broadway, 20th Floor, New York, NY 10019
SpecialSales@dk.com

Printed and bound in China

www.dk.com

Established in 1846, the Smithsonian is the world's largest museum and research complex, dedicated to public education, national service, and scholarship in the arts, sciences, and history. It includes 21 museums and galleries and the National Zoological Park. The total number of artifacts, works of art, and specimens in the Smithsonian's collection is estimated at 155.5 million.

This book was made with Forest Stewardship Council™ certified paper—one small step in DK's commitment to a sustainable future. Learn more at www.dk.com/uk/information/sustainability

The Solar System

4		
6	**THE SUN** ●	OUR STAR
10	**PARKER SOLAR PROBE** ●	SUN EXPLORER
14	**MERCURY** ●	CRATERED WORLD
18	**BEPICOLOMBO** ●	MISSION TO MERCURY
20	**VENUS** ●	DEADLY PLANET
24	**EARTH** ●	LIVING PLANET
26	**LIFE ON EARTH**	
30	**AURORAS** ●	DANCING LIGHTS
32	**INTERNATIONAL SPACE STATION** ●	COSMIC HOME
36	**THE MOON** ●	EARTH'S COMPANION
40	**APOLLO 11** ●	THE FIRST MOON WALK
44	**ARTEMIS** ●	BACK TO THE MOON
46	**MARS** ●	DUSTY MARS
50	**MARTIAN GIANTS**	
54	**PERSEVERANCE** ●	ROBOTS ON MARS
56	**CERES** ●	GIANT ASTEROID
58	**ASTEROIDS**	
60	**METEORITES** ●	SPACE TREASURE
64	**OSIRIS-REX** ●	ROCKY RENDEZVOUS
66	**JUPITER** ●	GAS GIANT
70	**JUPITER'S MOONS**	
72	**SATURN** ●	RINGED GIANT
76	**SATURN'S MOONS**	
78	**CASSINI-HUYGENS** ●	EXPLORING SATURN
80	**URANUS** ●	SIDE SPINNER
82	**NEPTUNE** ●	ICE GIANT
84	**PLUTO** ●	SMALL WORLD
86	**COMETS** ●	SPACE SNOWBALLS
88	**ROSETTA AND PHILAE** ●	COMET CHASER
90	**NEW HORIZONS** ●	MISSION TO PLUTO
92	**MILKY WAY** ●	HOME GALAXY

96 **Looking at the Universe**

98	**DEEP FIELD**	• DISTANT UNIVERSE
102	**JAMES WEBB SPACE TELESCOPE**	• TIME MACHINE
106	**AMAZING SPACE**	
108	**ETA CARINAE**	• TIME BOMB
110	**V838 MONOCEROTIS**	• LIGHT ECHO
112	**RHO OPHIUCHI**	• MULTICOLORED CLOUDS
114	**PILLARS OF CREATION**	• STAR NURSERY
118	**HUBBLE TELESCOPE**	• HUBBLE IN SPACE
122	**CRAB NEBULA**	• COSMIC DEBRIS
124	**HERBIG-HARO 211**	• BABY STARS
126	**BUBBLE NEBULA**	• HUBBLE'S BUBBLE
128	**HERBIG-HARO 46/47**	• STELLAR TWINS
130	**EXOPLANETS**	
132	**HERCULES GLOBULAR CLUSTER**	• GLITTER BALL
136	**ORION NEBULA**	• COSMIC FIRE
138	**HORSEHEAD NEBULA**	• SEAHORSE IN THE SKY
140	**RING NEBULA**	• DYING STAR
142	**BUTTERFLY NEBULA**	• STARLIT WINGS
144	**STEPHAN'S QUINTET**	• DANCING GALAXIES
146	**COLLIDING GALAXIES**	
148	**WHIRLPOOL GALAXY**	• GALACTIC MERGER
150	**NEUTRON STARS**	• SPACE SHAKERS
152	**BLACK HOLES**	• INVISIBLE FORCE

154	**GLOSSARY**
157	**INDEX**
160	**ACKNOWLEDGMENTS**

CONTENTS

IMPORTANT NOTICE
Observing the sun directly or through any kind of optical device can cause blindness. The authors and publisher cannot accept any responsibility for readers who ignore this advice.

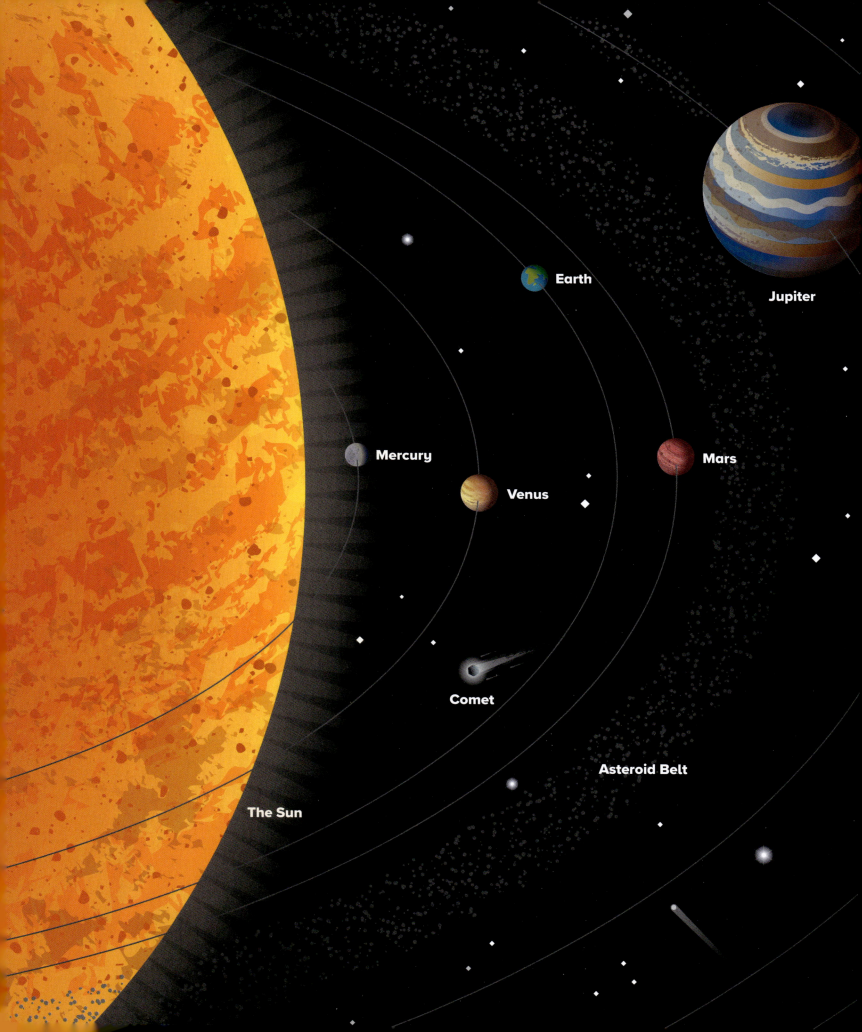

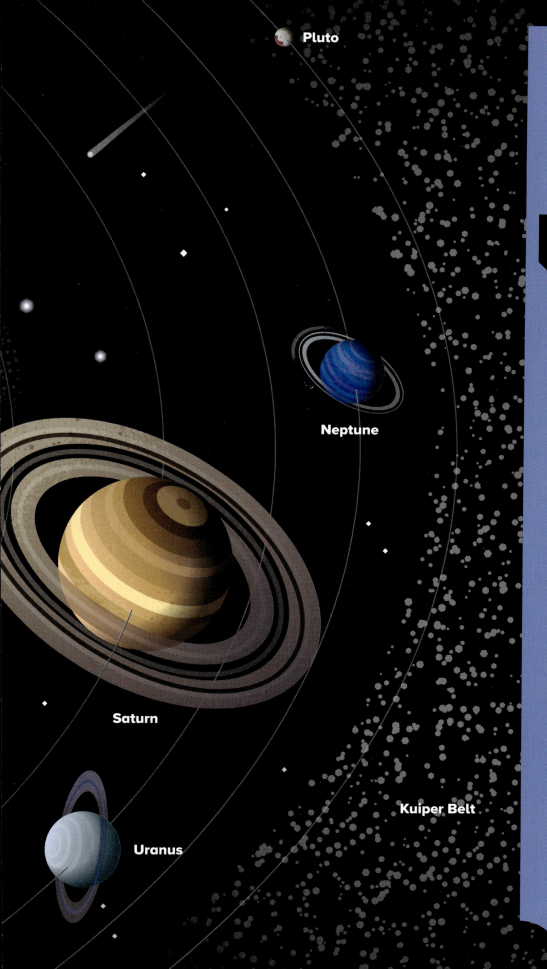

The Solar System

Earth, seven other planets, almost 300 moons, and billions of smaller objects orbit the sun. Together, these celestial bodies make up the solar system. Space probes are constantly investigating Earth's neighbors, bringing back new findings and stunning images.

6 • THE SUN

Our Star

YOU COULD FIT 1.3 MILLION EARTHS INSIDE THE SUN. But compared to other stars, our sun is an average-sized star—a glowing ball of mostly hydrogen and some helium, the two lightest elements in the universe. Its gravity keeps the planets, asteroids, and other objects in orbit around it. The light and heat that the sun gives off are what make life on Earth possible.

In a **MILLIONTH OF A SECOND,** the sun releases more energy than **EVERYONE ON EARTH** will consume in a year.

FIVE BILLION SUNS could fit inside the biggest known star in the universe— **UY Scuti.**

Jets of gas, called **prominences**, erupt from the sun.

INSIDE THE SUN

The sun's dense core is like a nuclear furnace, producing all the energy. This energy moves slowly through the radiative zone. In the convective zone, bubbles of hot gas rise to the surface, cool, and then fall back again toward the core. It can take more than 100,000 years for the sun's energy to travel from the core to the convective zone.

- Radiative zone
- Dense core
- Convective zone

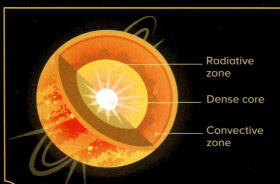

This false-colored, ultraviolet image of the **sun** was taken by NASA's Solar Dynamics Observatory. It shows jets of gas shooting out into space. These prominences are larger than Earth.

THE SUN

The sun's outer atmosphere, the **corona,** extends outward into space for millions of miles.

*It takes sunlight **EIGHT MINUTES** and **20 SECONDS** to reach Earth.*

DIAMETER

Earth: 7,926 miles / 12,756 km
Sun: 865,995 miles / 1,393,684 km

TEMPERATURE

SURFACE TEMPERATURE
9,930°F (5,500°C)

CORE TEMPERATURE
27 million°F
(15 million°C)

DISTANCE FROM EARTH

93 million miles
(150 million km)

AGE

The sun formed about 4.6 billion years ago from a huge cloud of dust and gas called a nebula—what was left over became the planets of our solar system.

MASS

The sun makes up 99.8 percent of the total mass of the solar system.

DEATH OF OUR STAR

When the sun runs out of fuel in about 5 billion years, it will grow to an immense size, becoming a red giant that swallows Mercury and Venus. Its outer layers will later blow away, leaving a core known as a white dwarf that will eventually fade.

White dwarf

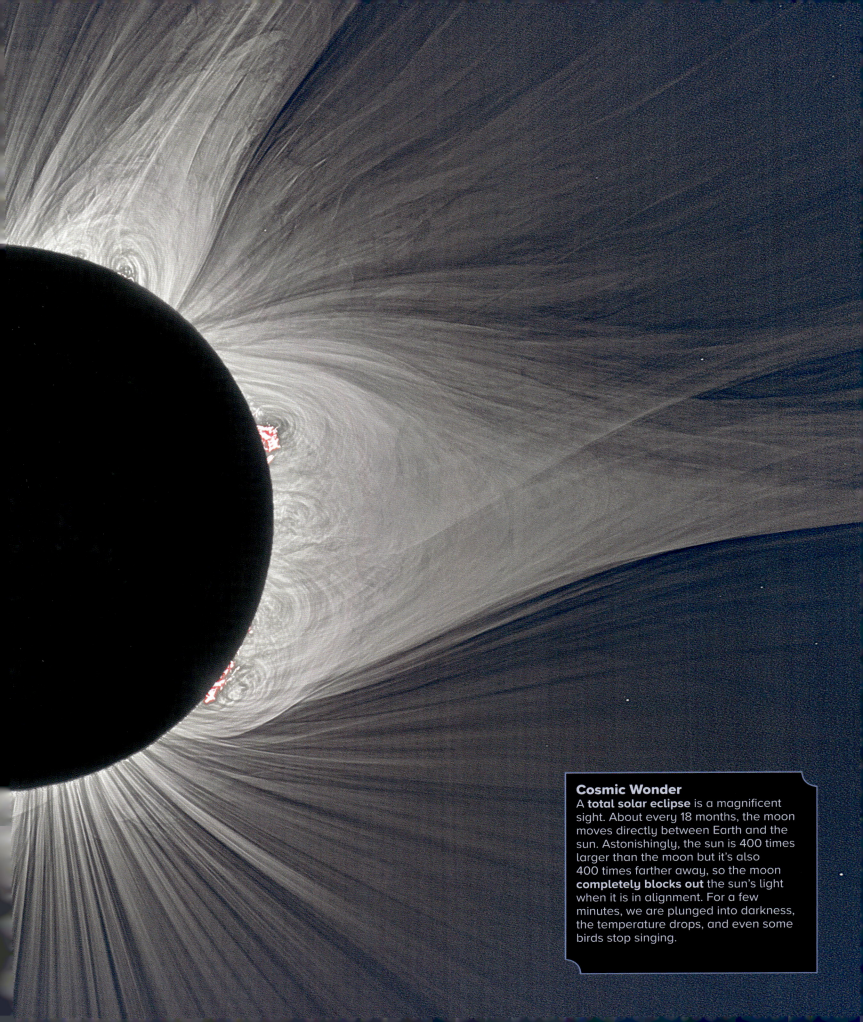

Cosmic Wonder
A **total solar eclipse** is a magnificent sight. About every 18 months, the moon moves directly between Earth and the sun. Astonishingly, the sun is 400 times larger than the moon but it's also 400 times farther away, so the moon **completely blocks out** the sun's light when it is in alignment. For a few minutes, we are plunged into darkness, the temperature drops, and even some birds stop singing.

PARKER SOLAR PROBE

LAUNCH DATE
August 12, 2018

MISSION DURATION

The mission is ongoing until 2025. The Parker Solar Probe will orbit the sun 24 times in total, with each orbit taking about 88 days.

RECORD BREAKER
The probe will come within 3.9 million miles (6.2 million km) of the sun. That's seven times closer to the sun than the previous record holders. These are NASA's two Helios probes, launched in 1974 and 1976.

TOP SPEED
125 miles (200 km) per second

SUN-SHIELD
The heat shield protects the instruments from the Sun. They are are kept cool at 85°F (29.5°C), while the corona temperature sizzles at around 2 million°F (1.2 million°C).

NEW FINDS

NASA's probe has taken images of comets and, for the first time, of Venus's surface in visible wavelengths.
Venus

SOLAR SCIENTIST
The probe is named in honor of American scientist Eugene Parker. In the 1950s, Parker predicted the existence of the solar wind and the spiral structure of the sun's magnetic field, now called the Parker spiral.

Sun Explorer

THE PARKER SOLAR PROBE IS THE FASTEST HUMAN-MADE OBJECT. It is also the first spacecraft to fly through the sun's outer atmosphere, the corona, and the first to gather never-before-seen images of the sun. The solar-powered probe is no bigger than a small car and can withstand the sun's blistering temperature and endless solar flares and radiation. Data gathered from the mission will help scientists understand how the sun affects space weather and its impact on Earth.

THE PARKER SOLAR PROBE makes its closest approach to the sun, as shown in this illustration. Its heat shield protects the probe from the sun's intense radiation.

This is one of three **magnetometers**, which are used to assess the sun's magnetic field.

At **TOP SPEED** the probe could travel from **NEW YORK** to **TOKYO** in less than a minute.

PARKER SOLAR PROBE ● 11

The **scientific instruments** are located behind the heat shield.

The 4½-in (11.5-cm)-thick carbon **heat shield** always faces the sun.

The front **antennas** work with the magnetometer at the back to measure the magnetic and electric fields around the Sun.

TOUCHING THE SUN

In 2021, the spacecraft flew through the sun's corona, marking the first time a probe had ever "touched" the sun. This illustration shows the probe flying through the corona, collecting information on the solar wind and the causes of the corona's extreme heat.

Corona | Solar wind | Parker Solar Probe

Scientists spent **60 years** developing the technology needed to build the **PARKER SOLAR PROBE.**

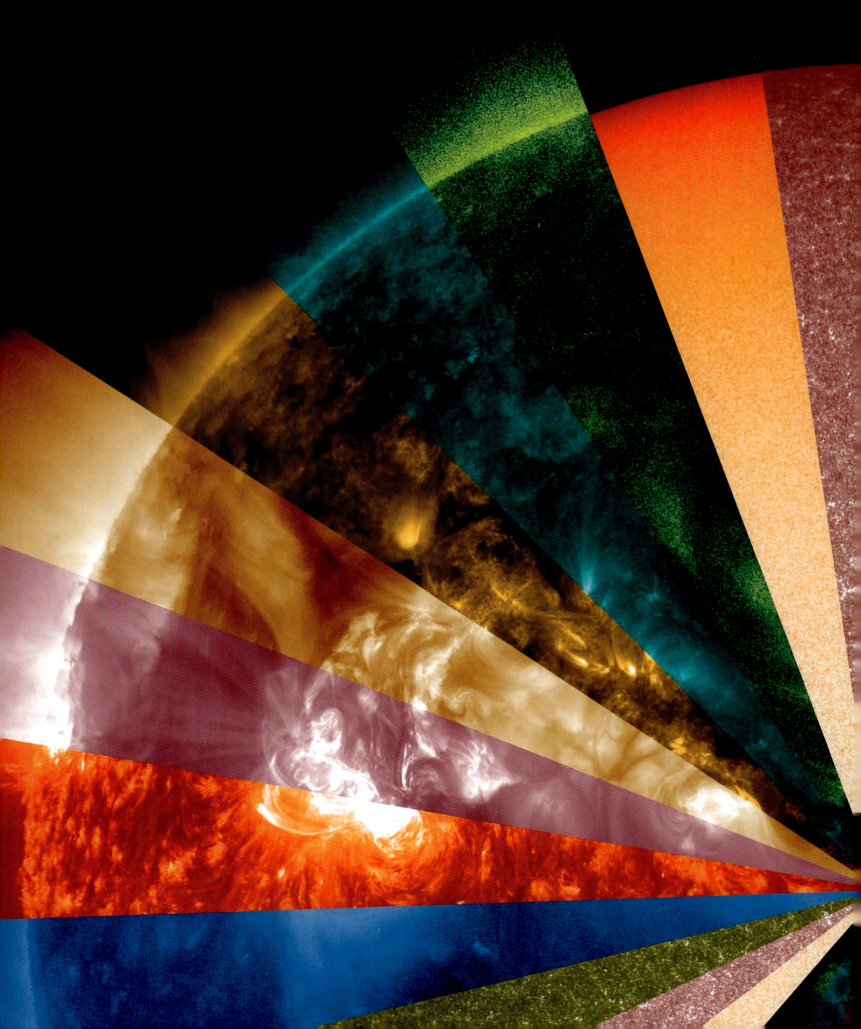

Seeing the Sun
The light we see from the **sun** is called visible light. However, the sun also emits light at **wavelengths** that we can't see. Scientists can study features of the sun in detail by using different wavelengths. This pattern shows an orange segment of the sun in visible light (right side of opposite page) followed by nine segments of wavelengths in false-colored ultraviolet, before the pattern repeats.

14 • MERCURY

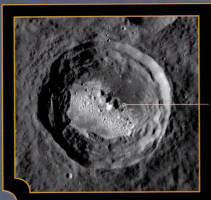

Some of the hollows are up to 5,250 ft (1,600 m) across.

MESSENGER
Between 2011 and 2015, NASA's MESSENGER spacecraft mapped 99 percent of Mercury's surface. It discovered features called hollows in some of the craters, which indicate that Mercury was once an active planet. It also discovered what may be water ice in the polar regions and unusually dark rocks on the surface, which may be made of graphite (carbon).

Mercury is covered in **ridges and cracks**, a result of the planet cooling and shrinking.

Cratered World

MERCURY IS THE FASTEST PLANET IN THE SOLAR SYSTEM. It orbits the sun at speeds of 29 miles (47 km) per second, giving it the shortest year of any solar system planet. Only slightly bigger than Earth's moon, it is the smallest planet and has the most extreme temperatures—blistering hot by day and bone-chillingly cold at night. Over millions of years, Mercury has been pounded by meteorites and comets, creating a scarred rocky world.

MERCURY spins very **slowly** so one day on this planet is **59 Earth days.**

Scientists think that **WATER ICE** might exist at the bottom of Mercury's **dark craters,** where sunlight doesn't reach.

MERCURY is a gray planet—the colors shown here represent the **chemical differences** that help scientists work out the composition of Mercury's rocks.

MERCURY 15

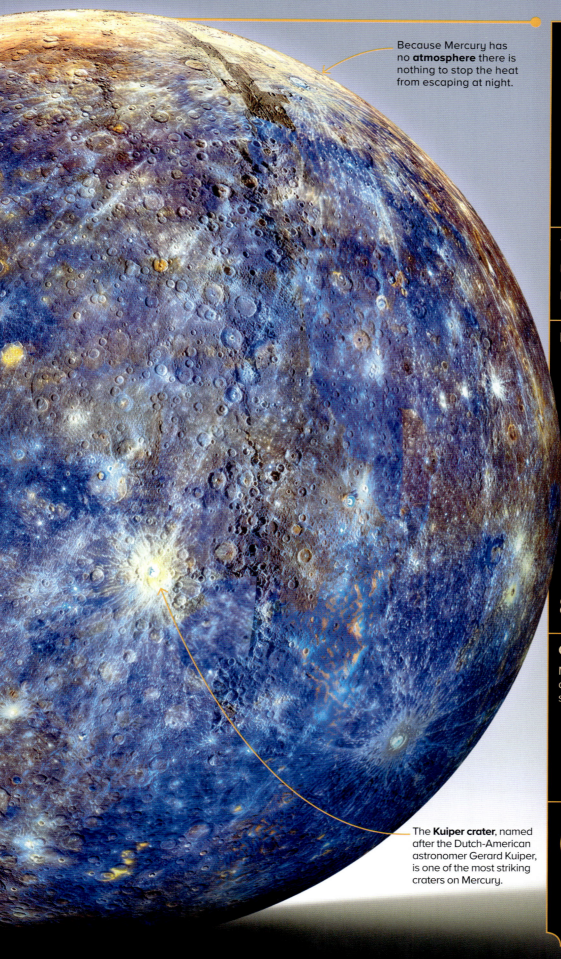

Because Mercury has no **atmosphere** there is nothing to stop the heat from escaping at night.

The **Kuiper crater**, named after the Dutch-American astronomer Gerard Kuiper, is one of the most striking craters on Mercury.

DIAMETER

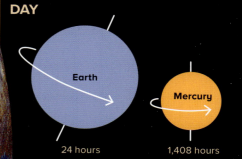

Earth — 7,926 miles / 12,756 km
Mercury — 3,032 miles / 4,879 km

YEAR

EARTH 365 days
MERCURY 88 Earth days

DAY

Earth — 24 hours
Mercury — 1,408 hours

TEMPERATURE

MINIMUM TEMPERATURE
-290°F (-180°C)

MAXIMUM TEMPERATURE
800°F (430°C)

ORBIT

Mercury has the least circular orbit of all the planets in the solar system.

MOONS

Mercury has no moons—its gravity is too weak and it is too close to the sun.

The sun's gravitational pull is too strong, resulting in a moon crashing into it.

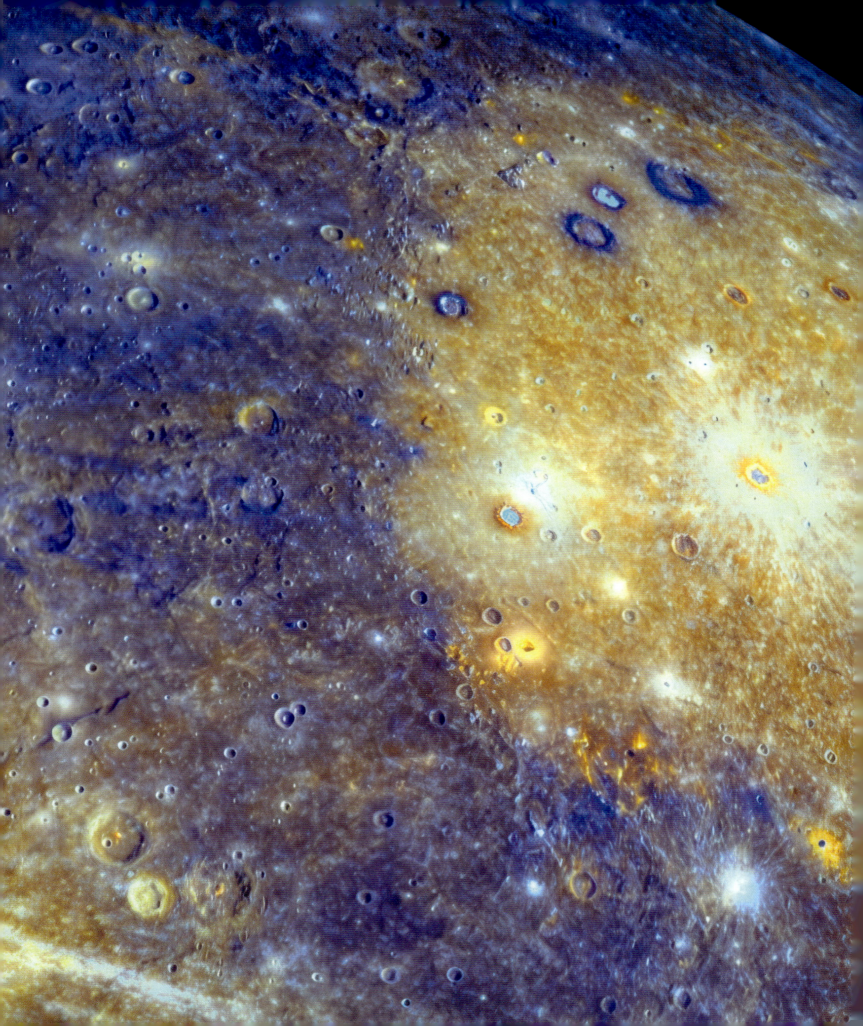

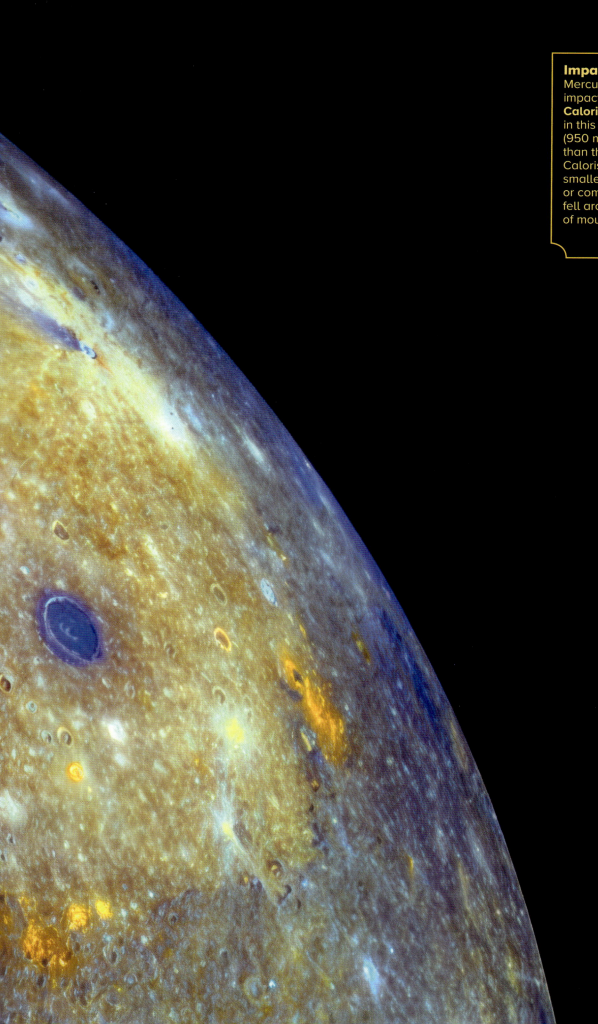

Impact Crater
Mercury is home to one of the largest impact craters in the Solar system—the **Caloris Basin** (visible as yellow-orange in this enhanced-color image). At (950 miles) (1,525 km) wide, it is larger than the state of Texas, in the US. The Caloris Basin is dotted with younger, smaller craters. Debris from the asteroid or comet collision that made the crater fell around the basin, creating a ring of mountains.

Mission to Mercury

MERCURY IS THE CLOSEST PLANET TO THE SUN. To study it in greater detail, the European-Japanese spacecraft BepiColombo was launched in 2018 on a seven-year journey to Mercury. When it arrives, in 2025, its two orbiters will collect data from different viewpoints. The orbiters will map the entire surface of Mercury and will also study the interior and the planet's magnetic field.

To withstand temperatures of more than 660°F (350°C) on the Sun-facing side, BepiColombo is protected by a covering made up of **50 layers of insulation**.

The **four solar-electric ion thrusters** propel the spacecraft.

THE SPACECRAFT

BepiColombo consists of three main parts. The Mercury Transfer Module is jettisoned before entering Mercury's orbit, while the two orbiters will separate once in Mercury's orbit.

1 Mercury Transfer Module This module carries BepiColombo to Mercury and is then ejected.

BEPICOLOMBO • 19

This **solar array** rotates continually to face the Sun. It supplies power to the Planetary Orbiter and also helps regulate the orbiter's temperature.

BEPICOLOMBO will reach Mercury in 2025. Once in Mercury's orbit, it will be on a year-long mission to collect data. Shown here is an artist's impression of the stacked spacecraft.

This **solar array** supplies power during BepiColombo's journey to Mercury.

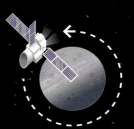

BEPICOLOMBO will orbit the Sun **18 times** before arriving in **MERCURY'S ORBIT.**

The spacecraft's **FLYBYS** enable it to reduce its speed by **7 km** (4 miles) per second.

2 Mercury Planetary Orbiter
The Planetary Orbiter will study the surface and interior of Mercury.

Heat shield

3 Mercury Magnetospheric Orbiter
This orbiter will study Mercury's magnetic field. The heat shield is ejected once in Mercury's orbit.

LAUNCH DATE
October 20, 2018

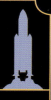

FLYBYS
BepiColombo will cover 5.3 billion miles (8.5 billion km), arriving at the planet in 2025. The journey involves nine flybys: one Earth flyby, two Venus flybys, and six Mercury flybys.

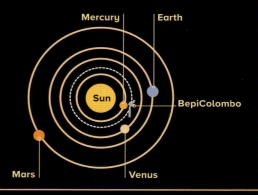

CLOSEST THE PLANETARY ORBITER GETS TO MERCURY'S SURFACE
298 miles (480 km)

MESSENGER
The first spacecraft to orbit Mercury was NASA's MESSENGER. It studied Mercury between 2011 and 2015, orbiting the planet 4,100 times and snapping almost 300,000 images. MESSENGER's data revealed that Mercury had shrunk by about 4 miles (7 km) since it formed 4.6 billion years ago.

BEPI
The spacecraft is named after Italian Professor Giuseppe (Bepi) Colombo who in 1970 correctly calculated how to get a spacecraft into Mercury's orbit.

20 • VENUS

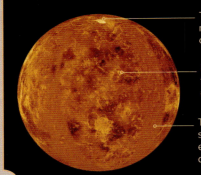

- The planet's highest mountain range is called Maxwell Montes.
- Many of the craters formed as a result of collapsed volcanoes.
- The surface is relatively smooth due to lava erupting from volcanoes and covering the surface.

BELOW THE CLOUDS
The image shown here of Venus was created from data sent to Earth by NASA's Magellan spacecraft. It shows what lies beneath the clouds—mountains, countless volcanoes, and a relatively smooth surface unlike the other rocky planets.

Deadly Planet

YOU WOULDN'T BE ABLE TO SURVIVE ON VENUS. It is a similar size and structure to Earth and has mountains and volcanoes. Scientists also think that Venus may once have harbored liquid water. But Venus also has dense clouds of deadly sulfuric acid, and its toxic atmosphere of carbon dioxide traps heat from the sun, making Venus the hottest planet in the solar system.

The **Venera 13** spacecraft holds the record for surviving on Venus—**127 MINUTES** before being crushed by the atmosphere.

Venus only has **MASSIVE CRATERS** on its surface—smaller meteorites burn up in its **THICK ATMOSPHERE.**

Venus's atmosphere is **100 TIMES THICKER** than Earth's.

VENUS'S surface is always covered by dense, swirling clouds. They can be seen in this image taken by Japan's Akatsuki orbiter, which reveals the planet's turbulent weather pattern.

VENUS 21

Venus's **clouds** extend 20–55 miles (30–90 km) above its surface.

Cloaked in a layer of clouds, only **10 percent** of the sunlight filters through to the planet's surface.

DIAMETER

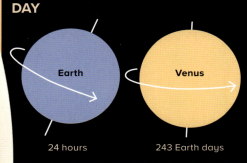

Earth — 7,926 miles / 12,756 km
Venus — 7,520 miles / 12,104 km

YEAR

EARTH **365 days**
VENUS **225 Earth days**

DAY

Earth — 24 hours
Venus — 243 Earth days

SLOWEST ROTATION

Venus has the slowest rotation of any planet in the solar system—a day on Venus lasts longer than its year, which is about 225 Earth days.

AVERAGE SURFACE TEMPERATURE

880°F (470°C)

PANCAKE DOMES

Unlike on Earth, the volcanoes on Venus are not super explosive so the lava flows slowly and starts to pile up, forming rounded shapes called pancake domes. These features are unique to Venus.

Fiery Planet
There are about **1,600 volcanoes** on Venus—more than on any other planet in the solar system. In 2023, scientists looking at radar images from NASA's Magellan mission found lava flowing from **Maat Mons**, Venus's largest volcano.

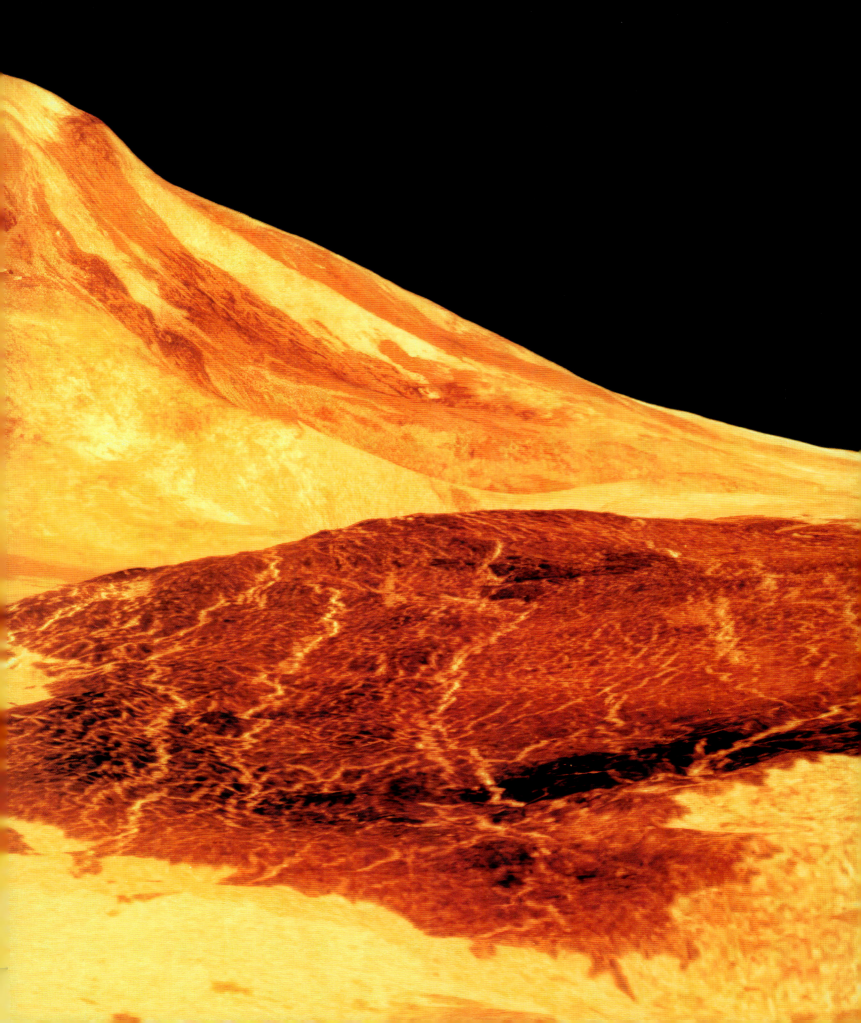

24 • EARTH

EARTH'S LAYERS

Earth formed about 4.6 billion years ago. It was a mass of molten liquid for millions of years. When it started to cool, it separated into the layers we see today. The deeper the layer, the hotter it is—at 10,800°F (6,000°C), the inner core is at least as hot as the surface of the sun.

Labels: Liquid oceans; Gaseous atmosphere; Inner core—solid ball of iron; Outer core—liquid iron; Mantle—rocks such as peridotite; Crust—mostly basalt and granite

Earth's thick atmosphere has **clouds and weather**.

Living Planet

EARTH IS A UNIQUE WORLD. Everything about our planet makes it the perfect place for supporting life as we know it. Earth is the only planet we know of that has liquid water on its surface. It is located in the habitable zone of the solar system, often called the Goldilocks Zone—where conditions are just right, not too hot and not too cold, for liquid water to exist. Our planet also has an atmosphere containing oxygen, and its magnetic field shields us from harmful radiation.

Some animals use Earth's **magnetic field** to help them **NAVIGATE** when migrating over long distances.

About **71 percent** of Earth's surface is covered in water.

Earth's **DAYS** are gradually getting longer as the **moon** slowly drifts away from Earth.

EARTH'S continents, oceans, and weather patterns can be seen in this beautiful image taken by NASA's remote sensing device MODIS on the Terra satellite, 435 miles (700 km) above Earth.

EARTH • 25

Earth's land is made up of continents that consist of **ancient rocks**, some of which are nearly as old as Earth itself.

DIAMETER

Earth

7,926 miles
12,756 km

YEAR

EARTH **365 days**

DAY

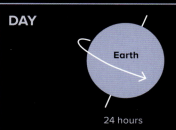

Earth

24 hours

TEMPERATURE

MINIMUM SURFACE TEMPERATURE
-128°F (-89°C)

MAXIMUM SURFACE TEMPERATURE
135°F (57°C)

ATMOSPHERE

The atmosphere consists of nitrogen (78%), oxygen (21%), and small amounts of other gases, including argon and carbon dioxide (just under 1%).

Nitrogen
Oxygen
Other gases

WATER

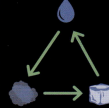

Earth is the only planet to have water that exists as vapor, liquid water, and solid ice on its surface.

TECTONIC PLATES

Earth's crust is split into tectonic plates. When these rub against each other, earthquakes happen.

26 • LIFE ON EARTH

DESERTS

Deserts are the driest habitats on Earth, with very little rainfall. From space, they can appear lifeless—as in this satellite image of sand and exposed rock (dark areas) in the Sahara. However, many organisms have adapted to survive here by storing seasonal rainfall, enduring dry periods, or gathering water from unexpected sources, including dew and fog.

Scientists estimate that Earth is home to over **8 MILLION SPECIES** of plants and animals.

RIVER DELTA

The essential role of water for living organisms is evident in Botswana's Okavango Delta. Each year, seasonal rains and flooding transform this dry desert into a lush expanse of grassy plains and lagoons, attracting vast herds of animals, including these African elephants.

ANTARCTICA

The frozen poles are also deserts, with their water locked away as ice. But even in Antarctica, some forms of life flourish. Colonies of emperor penguins can become so vast that they are visible to satellites in space.

CITY LIFE

By 2050, more than 68 percent of the world's people will live in urban areas. Cities such as Barcelona in Spain, shown here with its distinctive grid layout, face seasonal water shortages.

RICE TERRACES

Humans have disrupted the water cycle in many areas of the planet. Approximately 70 percent of the world's freshwater is used to water crops. Among these, rice grown in flooded fields called paddies is the most water-intensive crop.

LIFE ON EARTH • 27

RAINFORESTS
The Amazon rainforest receives as much as 10 ft (3 m) of rainfall every year, which helps make it one of the world's most biologically diverse habitats. Almost 400 billion trees thrive in the warm, wet climate. Each tree serves as a source of food and shelter for numerous other species.

OCEANS
About 70 percent of Earth's surface is covered in water, supporting 90 percent of its living creatures. Although most marine biodiversity is invisible from the surface, breaching pods of humpback whales remind us of the vast food chains that lie beneath the surface.

Life on Earth

WATER IS THE SOURCE OF ALL LIFE ON EARTH. From microscopic organisms to towering trees, they all share a reliance on water. Over the last 4 billion years, Earth's spectacular range of living organisms has profoundly reshaped the planet, changing its appearance even from space.

Destructive Force
Planet Earth is home to the most destructive tropical storms—**hurricanes**. These storms release as much energy as **10,000 nuclear bombs**. They form over warm oceans, reaching speeds of 155 mph (248 kph). Affected by the spinning Earth, vast spiral bands of rainclouds form around the calm eye of the storm. As they approach land, **winds, torrential rain, and storm surges** devastate coastal areas.

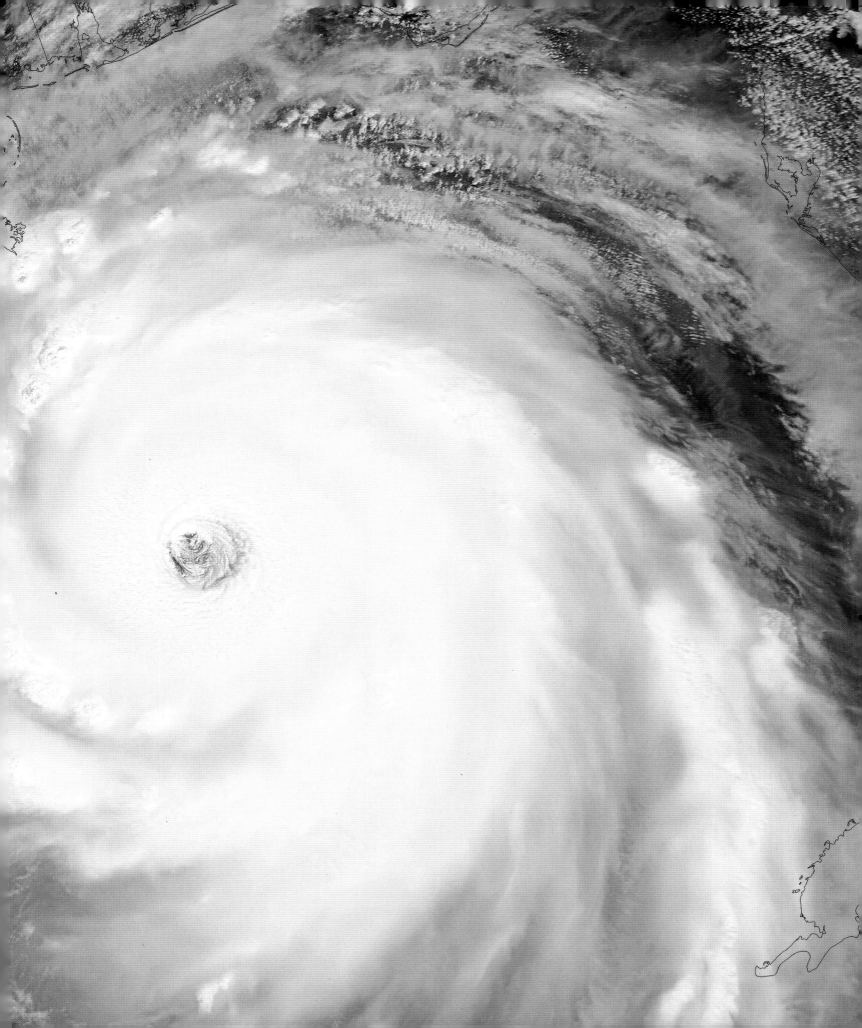

30 • AURORAS

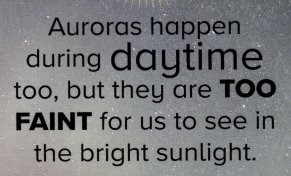

Auroras happen during **daytime** too, but they are **TOO FAINT** for us to see in the bright sunlight.

AN AURORA BOREALIS dazzles hauntingly over Lake Myvatn in Iceland. For a brief moment, the rays converge, creating a structured light display known as a corona aurora.

An aurora can extend up to **400 miles** (650 km) above Earth's surface.

Dancing Lights

AURORAS ARE THE MOST SPECTACULAR NATURAL LIGHT SHOWS. Greens and sometimes pinks, reds, and purples dance in the night sky, lasting for a few minutes or even for several hours. Early communities in Alaska and Canada saw them as dancing souls, flickering in the sky, and in Finland it was believed that they were the tails of fire foxes.

Most of the light is produced around **60 miles** (100 km) above Earth.

RING OF LIGHTS
Auroras generated at the North Pole are called the aurora borealis or northern lights, and those at the South Pole are known as the aurora australis or southern lights.

Aurora borealis

Aurora australis

AURORA COLORS
The colors of an aurora depend on the type of gas particles in Earth's atmosphere and the altitude at which charged particles from the sun collide with them.

GREEN
By far the most common color, green is caused by solar particles colliding with oxygen molecules at around 60–180 miles (100–300 km).

PINK
Flashes of pink occur when solar particles slam into hydrogen molecules in Earth's atmosphere at around 60 miles (100 km).

BLUE AND PURPLE
These colors are less common. They are produced when solar particles collide with nitrogen at around 60 miles (100 km) or less.

AURORAS

POWERING THE LIGHT SHOW
Earth is shielded by its magnetic field, which deflects most of the Sun's harmful electrically charged particles. But some solar particles are directed toward Earth's magnetic poles and collide with gas particles in the atmosphere, releasing energy as patterns of lights in the sky.

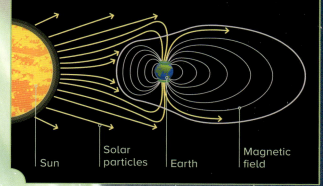

Sun | Solar particles | Earth | Magnetic field

Solar particles that produce auroras travel at speeds of up to **620 MILES** (1,000 km) per second.

SPACE AURORAS
There are auroras on other planets that have an atmosphere and a magnetic field.

Jupiter | Neptune

RINGSIDE SEAT
Astronauts on board the International Space Station (ISS) get a unique view of auroras, observing them as glowing arcs stretching across the atmosphere.

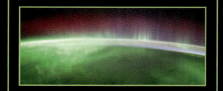

NIGHT-TIME MUSIC
Researchers in Finland have discovered that in certain weather conditions auroras made sounds—about 5 percent produced whooshing, crackling, or clapping sounds.

DISCOVERY
In 1896, Norwegian scientist Kristian Birkeland was the first person to describe what caused the glowing lights now known as auroras. But it took another 60 years before he was proven right.

32 • INTERNATIONAL SPACE STATION

TEAM EFFORT

Construction of the ISS involved the team effort of five national space agencies from the US, Russia, Canada, Europe, and Japan. The spacecraft now has 43 modules, which were launched from Earth on rockets and linked together in space. The roles of the modules vary from storage areas to laboratories.

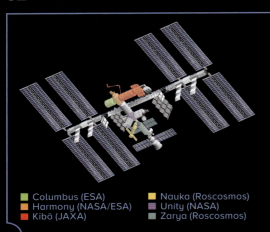

- Columbus (ESA)
- Harmony (NASA/ESA)
- Kibō (JAXA)
- Nauka (Roscosmos)
- Unity (NASA)
- Zarya (Roscosmos)

Cosmic Home

THE INTERNATIONAL SPACE STATION (ISS) IS THE LARGEST SPACECRAFT EVER BUILT. It took more than 40 missions and 10 years to assemble the modules in space. It orbits about 250 miles (400 km) above Earth's surface. Since its launch in 1998, more than 280 astronauts have visited the space station, carrying out science experiments designed to improve our ability to survive in space and establish permanent bases on other planets.

The ISS is powered by **solar panels** that convert sunlight into electricity. The solar panels rotate so that they always face the sun.

THE ISS is the second brightest object in the night sky after the moon. If you know when to look, you can see it at night—a luminous point of light that moves quickly across the sky.

LAUNCH DATE

The first module was launched on

November 20, 1998, and, with more sections added, the first crew arrived on

November 2, 2000.

SIZE

The ISS is **354 ft** (108 m) long and **243 ft** (74 m) wide, which is about the same length as a soccer field.

ORBITAL PERIOD

The ISS takes about 93 minutes to orbit Earth.

SPACEWALKS

More than 270 spacewalks have been made by ISS astronauts—a retractable 85 ft (26 m) braided steel rope keeps the astronauts attached to the ISS while they are carrying out repairs.

INTERNATIONAL SPACE STATION • 33

Orbiting Earth at a **speed** of about **5 miles** (8 km) per second, the astronauts see **16** sunrises and **16** sunsets every day.

Canadarm2 consists of seven motorized joints, allowing it to move in all directions.

The **Zvezda** module contains living quarters. It is attached to **Zarya**, which was the first module launched.

The **Soyuz** spacecraft stays docked to act as a lifeboat in emergencies and bring astronauts home.

LABORATORIES

Kibō is the biggest of the three laboratories. About the size of a bus, it has an exposed deck for carrying out experiments in space.

- Storage facility
- Robotic arm
- Communication system
- Exposed deck

CANADARM2

The 55-ft (17-m)-long robotic Canadarm2 is designed to work like a human arm, bending and turning to move equipment and astronauts outside the ISS.

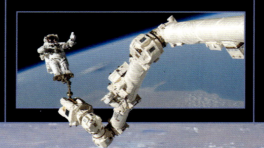

SPACE EXPERIMENTS

ISS astronauts have carried out more than 3,000 experiments, including growing vegetables and using imitation lunar soil to make glass, metals, and cement for future bases on other planets.

Astronauts grew lettuce in space.

Space Life
A rotating crew of about **six astronauts** live and work together aboard the ISS. As the space station orbits Earth, they experience **microgravity,** also known as weightlessness, as demonstrated here by Samantha Cristoforetti, European Space Agency (ESA) astronaut of Italian nationality. Astronauts have to exercise every day to prevent muscle and bone loss. Many experiments carried out on the ISS have helped improve our understanding of how our bodies work.

36 • THE MOON

CATASTROPHIC COLLISION

Most scientists today agree that the moon formed about 4.6 billion years ago when a Mars-sized object called Theia collided with a young, melted Earth. Material from this collision was propelled into space, clumping together and eventually forming the moon. This is why the rocks on the moon are very similar to Earth's.

THE MOON is a gray world to our eyes, but in this striking image it is shown in enhanced color to reveal its spectacular features.

With no atmosphere to protect it, the moon is often hit by meteorites, leaving it dotted with **impact craters**.

Earth's Companion

APART FROM EARTH, THE MOON IS THE ONLY PLACE IN THE SOLAR SYSTEM EXPLORED BY HUMANS. It is covered in craters, mountains, and dust. In the distant past, people kept track of long periods of time by watching the moon's changing phases—it takes about 29½ days for the moon to orbit Earth. The moon's gravity also pulls Earth's oceans toward it, causing the tides to rise and fall.

> The moon is **moving away from Earth** at a rate of about **1 1/2 IN** (4 cm) a year.

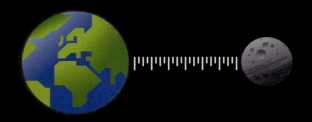

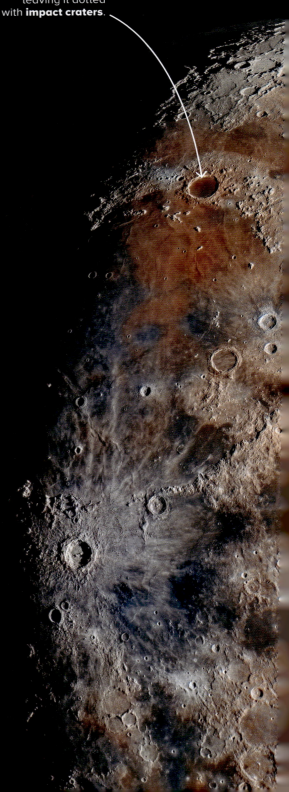

THE MOON • 37

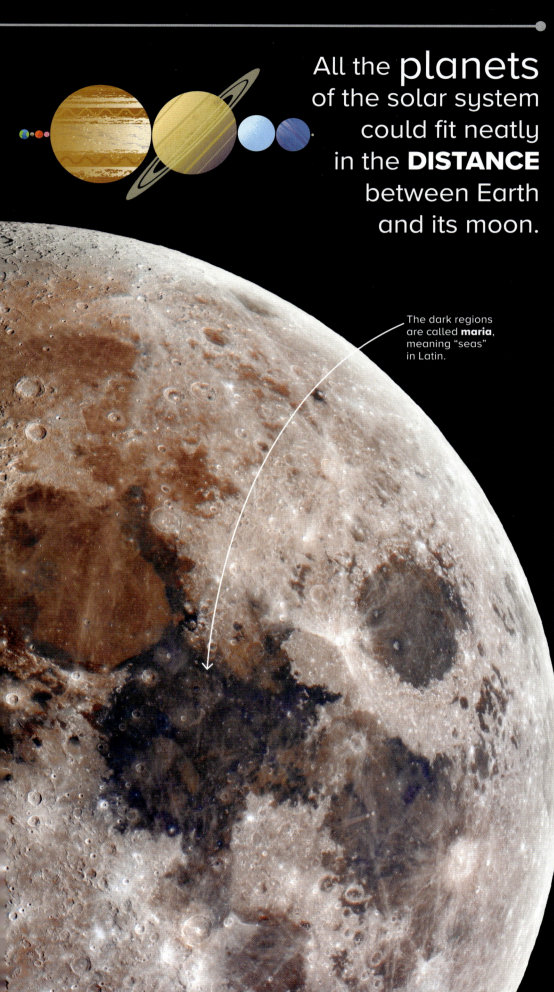

All the **planets** of the solar system could fit neatly in the **DISTANCE** between Earth and its moon.

The dark regions are called **maria**, meaning "seas" in Latin.

DIAMETER

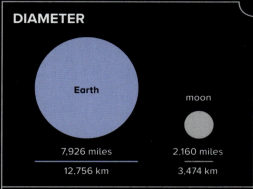

Earth — 7,926 miles / 12,756 km
moon — 2,160 miles / 3,474 km

DAY

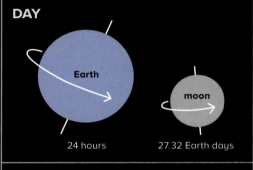

Earth — 24 hours
moon — 27.32 Earth days

AVERAGE DISTANCE FROM EARTH

238,855 miles (384,400 km)

TEMPERATURE

MINIMUM TEMPERATURE
-280°F (-173°C)

MAXIMUM TEMPERATURE
260°F (127°C)

FAR SIDE

The far side of the moon, which we don't see from Earth, has fewer seas (maria) than the near side. The seas are so called because astronomers once thought they were filled with water, but they are actually flooded with solid lava.

LOPSIDED

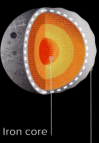

When the moon first formed, it was in a molten state. The side farther away from the hot Earth cooled more rapidly so more crust solidified there, making the moon lopsided.

Iron core
Thicker crust

Blood Moon

During a **lunar eclipse**, Earth's silvery-white moon turns a shade of copper-red. When the Earth moves between the sun and the moon, it casts a shadow across the moon's surface. But the moon doesn't disappear out of sight. Some red light from the sun gets through Earth's atmosphere and hits the moon, reflecting back into space and giving the eclipsed moon its nickname **"blood moon."**

40 • APOLLO 11

LAUNCH DATE
July 16, 1969

MOON LANDING DATE
July 20, 1969

TOTAL DISTANCE TRAVELED
953,054 miles
1,533,792 km

SATURN V
The Apollo spacecraft were launched by Saturn V rockets, which took a total of 24 astronauts to the moon.

APOLLO SPACECRAFT
Apollo 11 was made up of three parts: the Lunar Module Eagle, which touched down on the moon; the Command Module Columbia; and the Service Module, which supplied water and oxygen.

Lunar Module | Command Module | Service Module

BACK TO EARTH
The Apollo 11 astronauts collected samples of lunar dust and rocks. Upon their return to Earth on July 24, 1969, they had to declare the samples to customs. The flight number was recorded as Apollo 11 and the departure point was the moon.

ARMSTRONG and **ALDRIN** spent 21 hours and 36 minutes on the moon.

The First Moon Walk

NINE APOLLO CREWS MADE THE FANTASTIC JOURNEY TO THE MOON AND BACK, but Apollo 11 became famous as the first of six missions to successfully land astronauts on the surface. It was launched by a Saturn V rocket, the tallest, heaviest, and most powerful rocket of its time. Key moments of the eight-day expedition were watched live by hundreds of millions of people around the world.

THIS FAMOUS PORTRAIT of astronaut Edwin "Buzz" Aldrin on the lunar surface was taken by Neil Armstrong, commander of the mission and the first person to walk on the moon.

APOLLO LANDINGS
The six Apollo moon landings put 12 US astronauts on the moon. The last person to walk on the moon's surface was Harrison Schmitt in December 1972. The Artemis Program aims to return astronauts to the moon in 2026—more than 50 years since its last visitors.

- Apollo 11 Jul 69
- Apollo 12 Nov 69
- Apollo 14 Feb 71
- Apollo 15 Jul 71
- Apollo 16 Apr 72
- Apollo 17 Dec 72

Each Apollo landing explored a different lunar terrain.

APOLLO 11 • 41

Both Neil Armstrong and the Lunar Module are reflected in the **gold-plated sun visor** of Aldrin's helmet.

Aldrin's spacesuit was made of **12 synthetic materials with up to 21 layers**. It protected him from the harsh conditions on the moon, including extreme temperatures and ultraviolet radiation from the sun.

The **LUNAR MODULE** had just 25 seconds of fuel left when it landed.

Lunar Bootprint
When the **Apollo 11 astronauts** stepped onto the lunar surface in 1969, they left bootprints in the fine-grained soil. With no wind or rain to erode them, these prints are still visible. Lunar Module pilot **Buzz Aldrin** snapped this image of his boot within an hour of landing on the moon along with Neil Armstrong.

44 • ARTEMIS

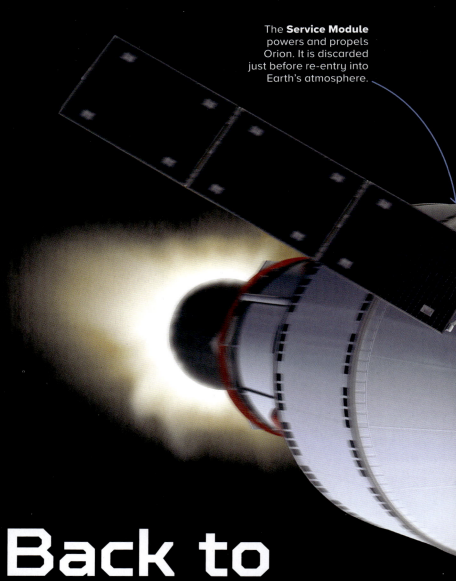

The **Service Module** powers and propels Orion. It is discarded just before re-entry into Earth's atmosphere.

ROCKET TO THE MOON

More powerful than the Saturn V rocket, which first took astronauts to the moon, the Space Launch System (SLS) will carry the Orion spacecraft and its crew into space. The rocket was successfully launched in 2022 as part of the Artemis I uncrewed mission.

Back to the Moon

In the future, astronauts will use the **MOON'S RESOURCES** to build a habitable base on the **LUNAR SURFACE.**

NASA'S ARTEMIS MISSION IS SENDING ASTRONAUTS BACK TO THE MOON. For the first time in over 50 years, astronauts will spend a week in the lunar South Pole region, which has never been explored by humans. The Artemis crew will conduct experiments aimed at establishing a future habitable base on the moon, serving as a stepping stone for missions to Mars and beyond.

ARTEMIS • 45

On its return journey, ORION re-enters the Earth's atmosphere at a speed of over **20,000 MPH** (32,200 kph).

The **Crew Module** provides space for four astronauts to live and work for up to 21 days.

DESIGNED TO TAKE HUMANS the farthest they've ever been into space, the Orion spacecraft consists of two main components—the Crew Module, which is a reusable capsule, and the Service Module, which contains support systems.

ARTEMIS MISSIONS

Led by NASA, the Artemis missions aim to establish regular trips to the Gateway Space Station, which will orbit the moon, and a base camp on the moon's surface.

○ **ARTEMIS I**
The first mission was an uncrewed test flight in 2022. Orion made two flybys of the moon.

○ **ARTEMIS II**
Planned for 2025, this mission will be the first crewed Orion flight, which will orbit the moon.

○ **ARTEMIS III**
This mission will land the first humans near the lunar south pole in 2026.

○ **FURTHER MISSIONS**
By 2030, Artemis missions will be supported by the Gateway Space Station.

LAUNCH ABORT SYSTEM (LAS)

Sitting atop Orion at launch, the LAS allows the Crew Module to be safely ejected from the main rocket if something goes wrong.

Launch Abort System

Crew Module

GATEWAY

NASA'S Gateway will be the first lunar space station. It will support Artemis missions, initially providing a base for astronauts before they visit the moon.

TEAMWORK

The names of almost 30,000 people whose work made the Artemis I mission possible were engraved on microchips and launched in Artemis I.

46 • MARS

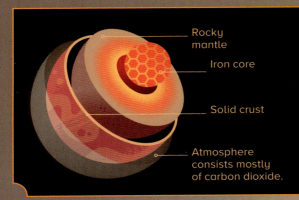

Rocky mantle
Iron core
Solid crust
Atmosphere consists mostly of carbon dioxide.

INSIDE MARS
Mars was a hot mass of molten rock that eventually cooled and solidified to form a solid crust. Beneath this crust lies a rocky mantle and a small, dense core that may be partly liquid. Unlike Earth, Mars doesn't have plate tectonics. So the Martian volcanoes, including Olympus Mons, continued to grow over millions of years in the same spot.

Olympus Mons hasn't erupted for millions of years.

Dusty Mars

SCIENTISTS HAVE SENT MANY ROBOTIC EXPLORERS TO MARS TO SEARCH FOR SIGNS OF PAST LIFE. With its striking Earthlike features—seasons, polar ice caps, canyons, and extinct volcanoes—the rust-red planet has captivated our imagination. But unlike Earth, it is not a habitable planet—it is a barren, bitterly cold world with an unbreathable atmosphere.

NASA'S **PERSEVERANCE ROVER** succeeded in making **OXYGEN** on **MARS**—a small step toward creating a breathable habitat for **HUMANS**.

Valles Marineris is a vast, deep canyon that is the width of the US.

OLYMPUS MONS, the biggest volcano in the solar system, is 2½ times the height of **QOMOLANGMA FENG** (Mount Everest).

Qomolangma Feng 29,031 ft 8½ in (8,848.86 m) high

Olympus Mons 72,000 ft (22,000 m) high

MARS 47

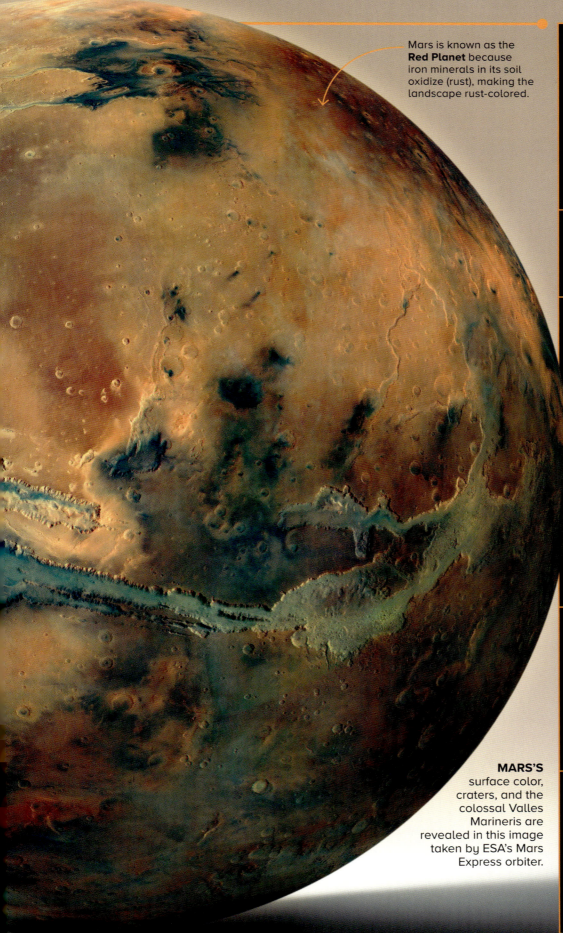

Mars is known as the **Red Planet** because iron minerals in its soil oxidize (rust), making the landscape rust-colored.

MARS'S surface color, craters, and the colossal Valles Marineris are revealed in this image taken by ESA's Mars Express orbiter.

DIAMETER

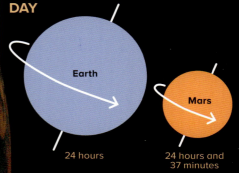

Earth — 7,926 miles / 12,756 km
Mars — 4,220 miles / 6,791 km

YEAR
EARTH **365 days**
MARS **687 Earth days**

DAY

Earth — 24 hours
Mars — 24 hours and 37 minutes

CLOUD-TOP TEMPERATURE

Minimum temperature
-225°F (-153°C)
Maximum temperature
95°F (35°C)

ORBIT

Mars orbits the sun in an elliptical shape (stretched oval)—more so than Earth.

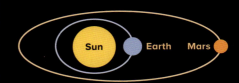

MOONS

Mars has two irregularly shaped moons—Deimos and Phobos. In Greek mythology, Phobos was the god of fear and Deimos represented terror. Phobos, which is closer to Mars, completes its orbit four times faster than Deimos.

Phobos

Deimos

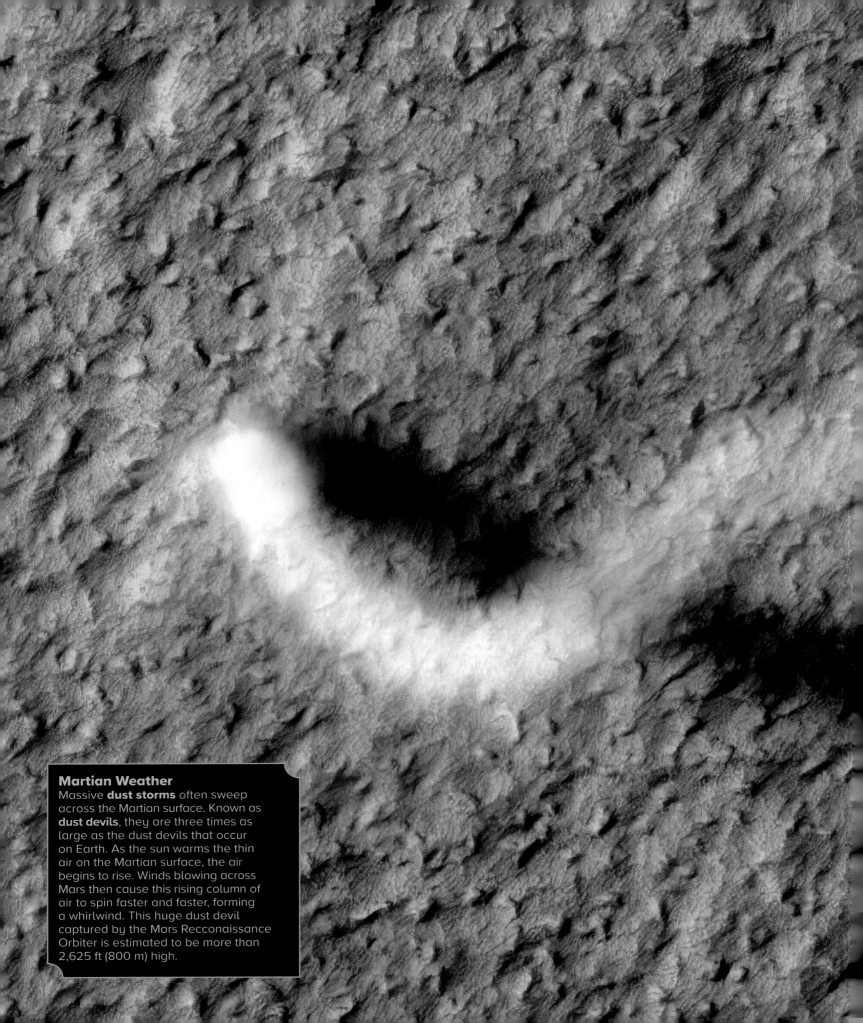

Martian Weather
Massive **dust storms** often sweep across the Martian surface. Known as **dust devils**, they are three times as large as the dust devils that occur on Earth. As the sun warms the thin air on the Martian surface, the air begins to rise. Winds blowing across Mars then cause this rising column of air to spin faster and faster, forming a whirlwind. This huge dust devil captured by the Mars Recconaissance Orbiter is estimated to be more than 2,625 ft (800 m) high.

50 • MARTIAN GIANTS

OLYMPUS MONS
This massive volcano would cover an area the size of France if it were located on Earth. At its summit, a vast caldera is visible, featuring several overlapping craters.

If the **frozen water** in Mars's soil melted, it would cover the planet in an **OCEAN** 115 ft (35 m) deep.

VALLES MARINERIS
This collection of connected canyons is ten times longer and five times deeper than Earth's Grand Canyon in the US. Valles Marineris formed when Mars's crust was stretched and ripped apart by lava bulging up under nearby Olympus Mons.

Martian Giants

PHOTOGRAPHS OF MARS'S SURFACE LOOK STRANGELY FAMILIAR. Many Martian landscapes—from steep-sided canyons to rippling dunes—are also found on Earth. However, even though Mars is much smaller, its features are often supersized compared to the versions on our planet.

SANTA MARIA CRATER
The Santa Maria Crater is the size of a sports stadium. Photographed by NASA's Opportunity rover in 2010, the site is shown here in false color, which helps reveal the features of the crater. Rocks line the rim while the sand dunes tumble in the middle.

MARTIAN GIANTS • 51

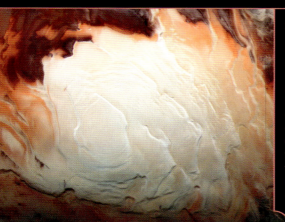

SOUTH POLE
Photos taken from space probes reveal that Mars has polar ice caps like Earth. The southern ice cap contains both water ice and frozen carbon dioxide—known as dry ice on Earth. The region also has irregular, dark features known as "spiders," formed when the dry ice turns back into gas in spring and escapes through the surface.

MARTIAN BLUEBERRIES
Scattered in several places, these tiny spheres that resemble blueberries are one of the clues that Mars once had liquid water on its surface. They are formed from iron-rich minerals that would have been dissolved in the water.

SAND DUNES
Sand dunes are common on Mars, but some have strange shapes compared to those on Earth. At the north pole, the tiny grains of dark volcanic sand are mostly covered by a layer of frozen carbon dioxide.

Water on Mars
Billions of years ago, **fast-flowing water** carved through the Martian landscape. Vast dried-up channels on the planet's surface have been discovered, as shown in this image taken by ESA's Mars Express orbiter. The channels indicate that Mars used to be very wet. What caused much of that water to disappear is still a mystery.

PERSEVERANCE

Perseverance **LANDED ON MARS** using a **JETPACK** called the Skycrane.

Robots on Mars

NASA'S CAR-SIZED PERSEVERANCE IS EXPLORING THE RED PLANET. It has been carrying out experiments ever since it landed on the Martian surface in 2021. Its aims include searching for signs of life and paving the way for future human missions to Mars. The rover has many cameras, two microphones—to capture sounds from Mars for the first time—and several other instruments to study the rocks, atmosphere, and weather on Mars.

This device can focus on the tiniest piece of rock before **analyzing** it with a laser.

The robotic arm supports the rover's "head," which contains five of Perseverance's **record-setting** 23 cameras.

This small **camera** can spot an object the size of a golf ball from about 82 ft (25 m) away.

Receiving commands from Earth, **PERSEVERANCE** continues to explore Mars for signs of past life. NASA's 3D model shown here depicts Perseverance collecting ancient rock samples.

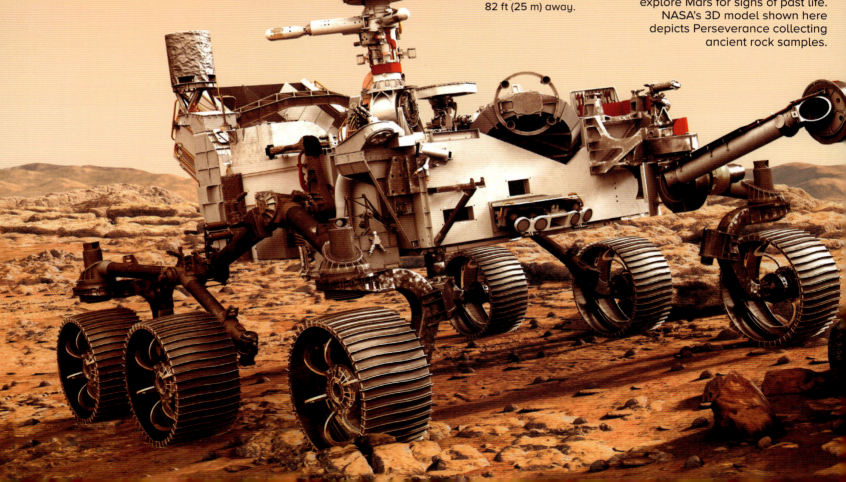

PERSEVERANCE ● 55

INGENUITY
Perseverance didn't travel to Mars alone. It carried Ingenuity, a small helicopter drone. Navigating Mars's rocky surface is slow, but flying Ingenuity allowed scientists to speed up exploration. Initially set for five test flights, the helicopter's success led to an additional 67 flights.

LAUNCH DATE
July 30, 2020

JOURNEY TIME
It took almost 7 months for the rover to travel from Earth to Mars, but just 7 minutes to land when it entered Mars's atmosphere.

1. Earth departure
2. Mars arrival
3. Mars departure
4. Earth sample return

TOP SPEED
Perseverance can travel at
0.07 mph (0.12 kph)—
slightly faster than a snail.

Perseverance has a **plaque** that is engraved with the **NAMES OF OVER 10.9 MILLION PEOPLE** who wanted to be part of the mission.

HI-SPEED HELICOPTER
Ingenuity spins its blades
40 times
a second.

POWER ON MARS
Perseverance uses nuclear fuel to create power and heat, while Ingenuity uses solar panels to generate electricity.

Ingenuity was the **first controlled aircraft** to fly on another planet. It was sent flight plans from Earth and then flew by itself.

LANDING SITE
Perseverance and Ingenuity are exploring an area of the Jezero Crater. About 3.5 billion years ago, this crater was flooded with water.

PARCELS FROM MARS
Armed with a small drill, Perseverance has been collecting rock samples the size of chalk sticks. These will eventually head back to Earth on a separate mission and may reveal if life ever existed on Mars.

56 • CERES

DIAMETER

Earth — 7,926 miles / 12,756 km
Ceres — 592 miles / 952 km

YEAR
- EARTH **365 days**
- CERES **1,682 Earth days**

DAY
- Earth — 24 hours
- Ceres — 9 hours and 4 minutes

INSIDE CERES

Scientists think that Ceres has an outer crust of ice and minerals. Underneath this is a mantle and possibly a core of water-bearing rocks.

- Crust
- Mantle
- Core

DAWN SPACECRAFT

It took NASA's Dawn spacecraft 7½ years to reach Ceres. In doing so, it became the first spacecraft to orbit two different solar system bodies—Vesta (2011) and Ceres (2015).

1. Earth departure
2. Mars flyby
3. Vesta arrival
4. Vesta departure
5. Ceres arrival
6. Mission end

LIQUID WATER

Radioactive rocks on Ceres provide enough heat to keep the buried water from freezing solid.

Giant Asteroid

CERES WAS THE FIRST ASTEROID TO BE DISCOVERED IN THE SOLAR SYSTEM. In 1801, while searching for planets, Italian priest and astronomer Giuseppe Piazzi spotted Ceres. Composed mainly of rock and metal, asteroids are found throughout the inner solar system but most lie within a ring between Mars and Jupiter known as the Asteroid Belt. Ceres is now classified as a dwarf planet.

CERES accounts for about a **THIRD** of all the material found so far in the Asteroid Belt.

CERES may consist of 25 percent **water**, making it a good place to search for **SIMPLE LIFE**.

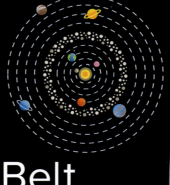

CERES 57

TOWERING GIANT
Shown here is the cryovolcano Ahuna Mons, which is no longer active. Almost half the height of Earth's tallest mountain, Qomolangma Feng (Mount Everest), it dominates Ceres's landscape. Rather than lava, cryovolcanoes erupt icy water containing salts and other minerals, leaving bright areas on the surface.

There are countless **small craters** on Ceres.

CERES'S rocky surface is shown in this view taken by Dawn from 240 miles (385 km) above the dwarf planet's surface. At the center is the Occator Crater—the bright spots within the crater may be traces of salty liquid.

Ceres is the **LARGEST** object in the **ASTEROID BELT**.

ASTEROIDS

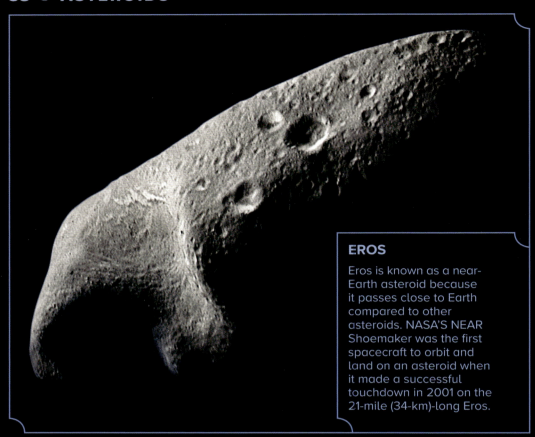

EROS
Eros is known as a near-Earth asteroid because it passes close to Earth compared to other asteroids. NASA'S NEAR Shoemaker was the first spacecraft to orbit and land on an asteroid when it made a successful touchdown in 2001 on the 21-mile (34-km)-long Eros.

ITOKAWA
Itokawa was the first asteroid to have a spacecraft collect material from it. This took place in 2005 when the Japanese spacecraft Hayabusa landed on the asteroid. The spacecraft collected more than 1,500 particles from Itokawa and returned them to Earth in 2010. Since then, scientists have been studying the particles to learn about the minerals found in asteroids.

Asteroids

SOME ASTEROIDS ARE THE SIZE OF SMALL CITIES. A few of these space rocks even have their own moons. Asteroids are the rubble left over from the creation of the planets. Thousands have been tracked, providing scientists with information about how the planets formed. They may also provide the missing link as to how life started on Earth. A rich source of minerals, metals, and water, asteroids could one day be used for establishing habitable bases on other planets.

About 66 million years ago, an **ASTEROID** bigger than Qomolangma Feng (Mount Everest) slammed into **Earth,** leading to the extinction of the **DINOSAURS.**

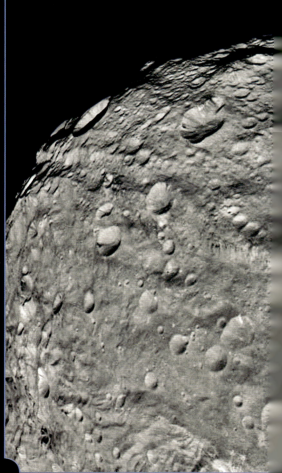

ASTEROIDS • 59

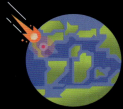

About every 2,000 years, an **ASTEROID** the size of a soccer field will slam into Earth.

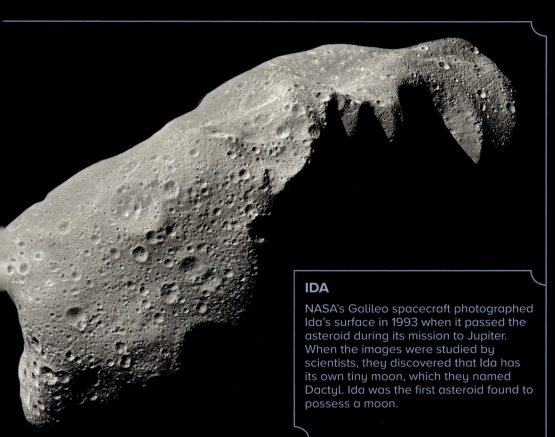

IDA
NASA's Galileo spacecraft photographed Ida's surface in 1993 when it passed the asteroid during its mission to Jupiter. When the images were studied by scientists, they discovered that Ida has its own tiny moon, which they named Dactyl. Ida was the first asteroid found to possess a moon.

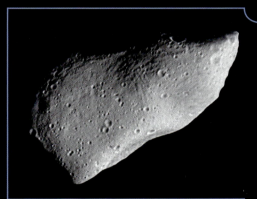

GASPRA
This asteroid rotates counterclockwise once every seven hours as it orbits the sun. It is only 11 miles (18 km) long but this view, taken by NASA's Galileo spacecraft, shows more than 600 craters.

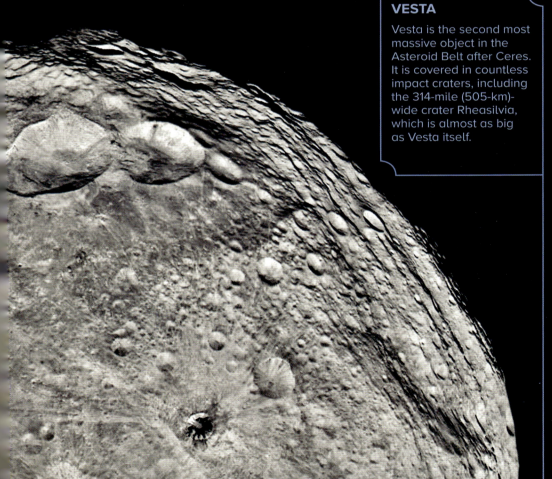

VESTA
Vesta is the second most massive object in the Asteroid Belt after Ceres. It is covered in countless impact craters, including the 314-mile (505-km)-wide crater Rheasilvia, which is almost as big as Vesta itself.

RYUGU
The Japanese spacecraft Hayabusa2 arrived at Ryugu in 2018, collecting samples to return to Earth. Scientists discovered organic molecules in the samples—these molecules are the building blocks of life on Earth.

60 • METEORITES

TYPES OF METEORITE
Three main types of meteorite are found on Earth. Most common are stony meteorites, made mostly of silicate rock. Iron meteorites are mainly iron-nickel, and very magnetic. Rarest of all are stony-iron meteorites—like the Fukang meteorite—with equal quantities of silicate minerals and metal.

Stony meteorite   **Iron meteorite**   **Stony-iron meteorite**

Space Treasure

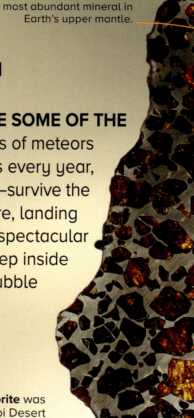

The large crystals are **olivine**, which is thought to be the most abundant mineral in Earth's upper mantle.

ROCKS THAT FELL FROM SPACE ARE SOME OF THE RAREST ON EARTH. Although millions of meteors light up the night sky as shooting stars every year, only a tiny fraction—several thousand—survive the hypersonic trip through the atmosphere, landing on Earth's surface as meteorites. This spectacular example is thought to have formed deep inside a planetesimal—a massive clump of rubble left over from the formation of the sun.

The Fukang meteorite was discovered in China's Gobi Desert in 2000. It is a pallasite—a type of stony-iron meteorite. This crescent-shaped slice has been polished to show off the sparkling crystals.

AGE
At 4.5 billion years, space rocks like the Fukang meteorite are almost as old as the solar system itself.

SIZE
When first discovered, the Fukang meteorite weighed about a ton, making it the third-largest pallasite ever found. Over time, it has been cut into pieces to be studied and sold.

ORIGINS
Most meteorites that land on Earth formed in the Asteroid Belt between Mars and Jupiter. They would have been part of asteroids that were fractured into pieces by collisions with other asteroids.

SPACE TRAVELERS
Scientists have identified around 35,000 near-Earth asteroids. Most of them are less than 0.6 miles (1 km) in diameter.

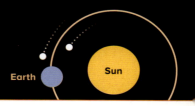

METEORITES • 61

Pallasites are among the rarest and most valuable METEORITES, accounting for just one in every 500 discoveries.

In some places, thin **"veins" of metal** wind their way through clusters of olivine crystals.

The olivine crystals are embedded in **iron-nickel**, thought to be the main elements in Earth's core.

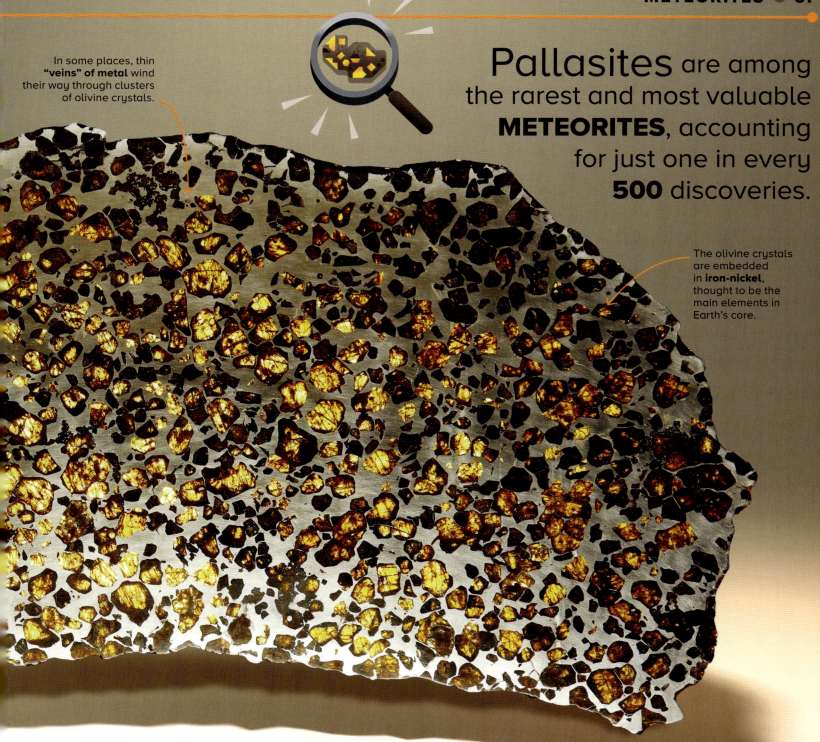

ROCK NAMES
The name of a space rock changes as it gets closer to Earth. In space, it is called a meteoroid; as it enters the atmosphere, it becomes a meteor; and if it reaches the ground, it is known as a meteorite.

NAMING METEORITES
Meteorites are named after the place where they are found. The family of pallasites that this meteorite belongs to is named after Peter Pallas, a German scientist who went to study a pallasite found in Siberia in the 1770s. He did not believe local people who said it had fallen from space, although they turned out to be right.

GEMSTONES
Pure and transparent olivine crystals are known as peridot. These precious stones have been treasured since ancient times, including by the ancient Egyptians, who referred to peridot as the "gem of the sun."

Barringer Crater
About 50,000 years ago, a **meteor** hurtled toward Earth. It struck what is now Arizona, US, shattering 175 million tons (160 million tonnes) of rock. This impact created the **Barringer Crater**, also known as Meteor Crater. It is one of the best-preserved impact craters on Earth. It has been used by NASA to train astronauts for the Apollo missions.

Rocky Rendezvous

NASA'S OSIRIS-REx MISSION ACHIEVED AN AMAZING AND AMBITIOUS GOAL. Hurtling through space, it collected a sample of rock from an asteroid, named Bennu, and then successfully returned the sample to Earth. Bennu is thought to have formed early in the existence of the solar system. By analyzing the rock sample, scientists can understand more about how the solar system formed.

BENNU has a 1 in 1,750 chance of **striking Earth** in the late 22nd century.

Bennu has a surprisingly active surface, often throwing loose rocks into space.

BENNU

Named after an ancient Egyptian mythological bird, Bennu is roughly diamond-shaped with an average diameter of about 1,640 ft (500 m). The asteroid is considered potentially hazardous because its orbit brings it close to Earth's. When OSIRIS-REx approached Bennu, it captured images of the asteroid, enabling NASA to select a sampling site for the touchdown. This image was taken by OSIRIS-REx from about 15 miles (24 km) away.

OSIRIS-REx

OSIRIS-REx traveled about **4 billion miles** (7 billion km) to return its sample to Earth.

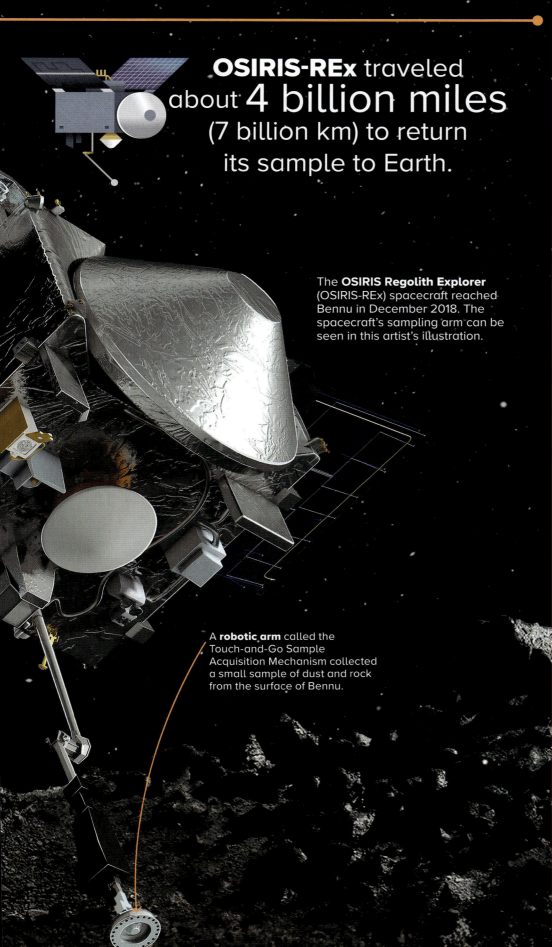

The **OSIRIS Regolith Explorer** (OSIRIS-REx) spacecraft reached Bennu in December 2018. The spacecraft's sampling arm can be seen in this artist's illustration.

A **robotic arm** called the Touch-and-Go Sample Acquisition Mechanism collected a small sample of dust and rock from the surface of Bennu.

LAUNCH DATE
Sept 8, 2016

SAMPLE TIME

The sampling head touched Bennu's surface for just six seconds. Most of the samples were taken within the first three seconds.

SAMPLE RETURN CAPSULE
In September 2023, the Sample Return Capsule re-entered Earth's atmosphere at an astonishing 27,650 mph (44,500 kph) before landing in a desert in Utah, US.

ROCKY RECOVERY

The capsule contained about 120 g (4⅓ oz) of dust and rock – more than twice the amount scientists had expected.

ANALYSIS
The samples revealed the presence of organic molecules and water-bearing minerals, which are needed for life.

NEXT MISSION
The spacecraft is now on a new mission, called OSIRIS Apophis Explorer (OSIRIS-APEX), to study the near-Earth asteroid Apophis.
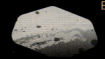

SIMILAR MISSIONS
The Japanese Hayabusa missions collected and returned samples from the asteroids Itokawa (2010) and, as shown here, Ryugu (2020).

JUPITER

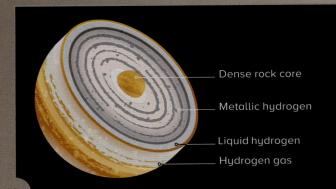

BALL OF GAS
Jupiter does not have a solid surface. Its atmosphere consists mostly of hydrogen gas and some helium. Beneath this, the pressure is so intense that it transforms the hydrogen into liquid. The dense core is surrounded by metallic hydrogen, which behaves like a liquid metal.

Gas Giant

JUPITER IS A COLOSSAL PLANET. All the other planets of the solar system could fit inside it and there would still be room to spare. Made of gas, it contains twice as much material as in all the other planets combined. Everything about Jupiter is immense, including its storms—many are the size of Earth. Some crash into each other and form even bigger storms.

JUPITER spins so fast that it isn't **round**—it is shaped like a **SQUASHED BALL**, bulging slightly in the middle.

JUPITER has a constant supply of charged particles that power its **NEVER-ENDING** auroras.

Jupiter's **south pole** is dominated by storms that swirl clockwise. They appear to change size, shape, and even their color.

JUPITER'S spectacular marblelike features are brought to life in this enhanced-color image taken by NASA's Juno spacecraft.

JUPITER • 67

Clouds of gas arise from the planet's interior, forming colorful bands that stretch across the surface.

SIZE

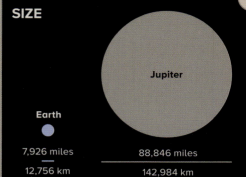

Earth — 7,926 miles / 12,756 km
Jupiter — 88,846 miles / 142,984 km

YEAR

EARTH **365 days**
JUPITER **4,332 Earth days**

DAY

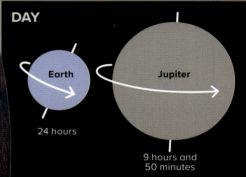

Earth — 24 hours
Jupiter — 9 hours and 50 minutes

CLOUD-TOP TEMPERATURE

-162°F (-108°C)

COLOSSAL STRIKE

In 2009, Jupiter was hit by an asteroid or comet that left a dark scar on the side of the planet. The impact was the equivalent of several thousand nuclear bombs exploding, and the scar it created is the size of the Pacific Ocean—Earth's largest ocean.

JET STREAM

A jet stream swirls around Jupiter's equator at speeds of 320 mph (515 kph). This is the equivalent to twice the speed of a Category 5 hurricane—the most destructive hurricane on Earth.

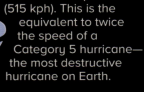

Red Storm
Jupiter's **Great Red Spot** is the largest storm in the solar system. Spanning 10,159 miles (16,350 km), it is wider than Earth's diameter and has been raging for around **190 years**. Smaller storms get drawn into its powerful spinning vortex—they either merge to fuel the massive storm or get torn apart by its turbulent winds.

JUPITER'S MOONS

IO

Jupiter's third-largest moon Io is dotted with hundreds of active volcanoes, such as Culann Patera (above). Lava flows of different ages surround the volcano's caldera (crater).

CALLISTO

Unlike Io, there are no active volcanoes on Callisto. The moon's surface is covered in rocks and ice, as well as ancient craters caused by billions of years of meteorite strikes. Many of the craters have multiple rings, like the frozen ripples of a stone dropped into a pond. Scientists think there may be a layer of salty liquid beneath the surface.

Jupiter's Moons

JUPITER HAS ALMOST 100 MOONS IN ORBIT AROUND IT. The four largest—known as the Galilean moons—are as unique and fascinating as any planet. Surface features suggest that three of these large moons—Ganymede, Callisto, and Europa—have vast underground oceans of salty water, making them a focus for scientists seeking signs of life outside Earth. The other Galilean moon—Io—is the most volcanic world in the solar system.

Jupiter's **GALILEAN MOONS** are named after Italian scientist **GALILEO GALILEI**, who discovered them in **1610.**

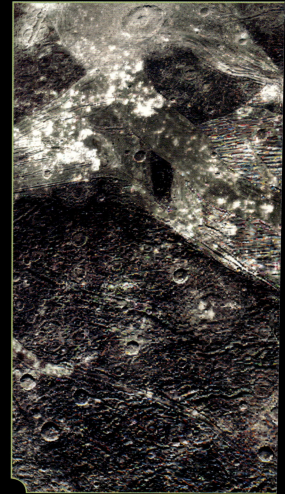

JUPITER'S MOONS • 71

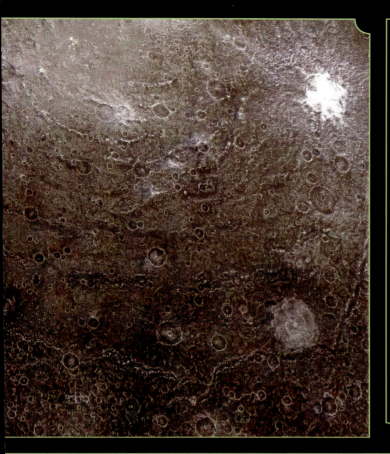

EUROPA
The cracks and ridges crisscrossing Europa are signs that a vast liquid ocean lies beneath this moon's frozen crust. Tides in this ocean cause the crust to break apart, with pieces drifting into new positions before refreezing. The darker orange areas (right) reveal where newer ice has seeped up from below to seal the cracks.

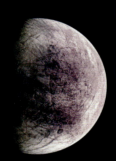

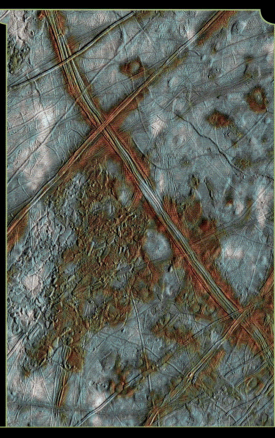

GANYMEDE
Much of Ganymede's surface is covered in strange grooves and ridges, some of which run for thousands of miles. There are also much smoother areas, suggesting that tectonic forces affect Ganymede's icy crust.

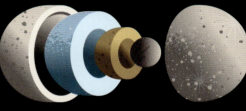

Ganymede is **MUCH SMALLER** than Earth, but the **oceans** under its icy crust may hold more water than Earth's as they are **30 times deeper.**

Ringed Giant

SATURN IS A SPECTACULAR PLANET. Storms rage for months on end, unleashing powerful lightning. Its dazzling ring system is by far the biggest in the solar system, and orbiting the gas giant is a colossal collection of 146 moons. Despite being almost as big as Jupiter, it contains much less material—if you happened to have a solar system-sized bath, Saturn would float on the water.

SATURN AND ITS RING SYSTEM are captured by NASA's Cassini spacecraft in this stunning image. Different colors have been used to show the differences in the size of the icy particles that make up the rings.

DIAMETER

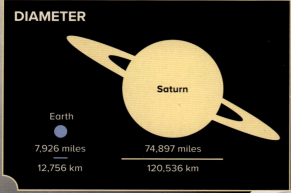

Earth — 7,926 miles / 12,756 km
Saturn — 74,897 miles / 120,536 km

YEAR

EARTH **365 days**
SATURN **10,747 Earth days**

CLOUD-TOP TEMPERATURE

-218°F (-139°C)

DAY

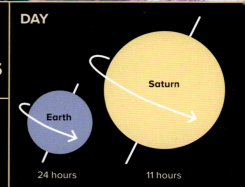

Earth — 24 hours
Saturn — 11 hours

SATURN 73

Green shows regions where the particles in the rings are **less than 5 cm (2 cm)** across.

HEXAGONAL STORM
Towering above Saturn's north pole is an unusual storm shaped like a hexagon, which has been raging for decades. The storm is twice the size of Earth and extends 60 miles (100 km) into Saturn's atmosphere.

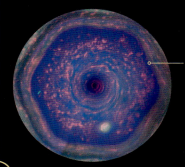

The hurricane spins counterclockwise while some of the smaller hurricanes within the hexagon spin clockwise.

About every **30 YEARS** a giant storm three times the size of Earth rages across Saturn's surface.

It would take you **345 DAYS** to travel across Saturn's **rings** at 30 mph (50 kph).

Purple shows regions where there are **no particles less than 2 in (5 cm)** across.

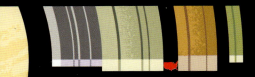

RINGS
Saturn's rings include several gaps caused by the gravitational pull of its moons. The largest, the Cassini Division, is 2,920 miles (4,700 km) wide—big enough to fit the US inside it.

USA

RINGED PLANETS
Jupiter, Uranus, and Neptune all have rings but they are harder to spot and contain far less material than Saturn's rings.

Jupiter   Uranus   Neptune

RING MATERIAL
Saturn's rings are made of billions of pieces of ice, rocks, and dust—thought to be fragments of comets, asteroids, or moons. Some are house-sized; others are no bigger than ice cubes.

Luminous Rings
Lit by the Sun, Saturn's **rings dazzle** in space in this stunning image taken by NASA's Cassini spacecraft. Scientists think the ring system formed between 10 million and 100 million years ago, with Saturn's gravity preventing the ring fragments from forming a moon. The main rings span **174,000 miles** (280,000 km) and are astonishingly thin, measuring no more than **33 ft** (10m) deep.

Saturn's Moons

SATURN HAS THE MOST MOONS OF ANY PLANET IN THE SOLAR SYSTEM. This huge collection of more than 140 moons has some unusual members too. They range in size from tiny objects to some of the largest moons discovered around any planet. The first of Saturn's many moons to be spotted was Titan in 1655. More than 360 years later, scientists are still finding new moons.

Scientists believe that **two** large **icy** moons smashed into each other, creating Saturn's rings and many of its other **MOONS**.

ENCELADUS
Enceladus is one of the most reflective objects in the solar system. This is because it is covered in a thin layer of ice. Scientists think it may be one of the few worlds that has an ocean of liquid water beneath its surface. It also has more than 100 cryovolcanoes, which constantly spray ice and other material onto its surface. Some of this icy material is hurled into space and ends up in Saturn's outer ring.

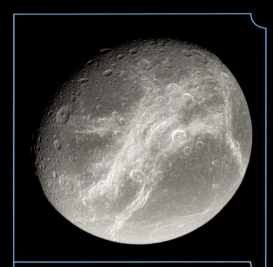

DIONE
Dione's icy surface is pitted with craters and vast canyons and cliffs. The moon orbits Saturn every 2.7 days, within the planet's outer ring, and is accompanied by two small irregular moons, Helene and Polydeuces.

HYPERION
Not all of Saturn's moons are spherical. Hyperion is the largest of the irregular moons. Deep craters from collisions give Hyperion its unusual spongelike appearance. About 40 percent of the moon is empty space, with hollows inside it. Because of its odd shape, Hyperion tumbles chaotically around Saturn on its 21-day orbit.

PHOEBE
Unlike most of Saturn's moons, Phoebe rotates counterclockwise on its 18-month orbit. Material from objects impacting this moon have added to Saturn's biggest ring and to the nearby moon Iapetus. The dark surface of Phoebe is covered in massive craters.

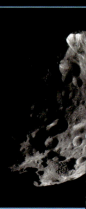

SATURN'S MOONS • 77

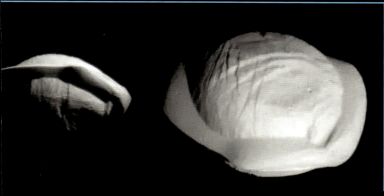

PAN
This unusual-looking moon has collected material from Saturn's rings, which has now formed a large ridge around the moon. Pan orbits the gas giant within its rings and is known as a shepherd moon because it "herds" material within the gap.

IAPETUS
Iapetus is a peculiar-looking moon with one side bright and the other very dark. The exact cause of this is unknown. Some scientists suggest the dark material comes from another moon and falls onto Iapetus's surface, while others think that volcanic eruptions from beneath the moon's surface could be responsible for the dark material.

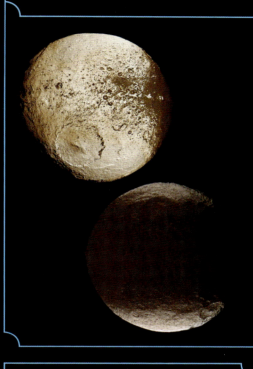

TITAN
Saturn's largest moon Titan is the second-largest in the solar system after Jupiter's Ganymede, which is only about 2 percent bigger. Titan has a thick atmosphere, making it look hazy. It also has liquid rivers of ethane and methane flowing across its surface. This image of Titan is a composite infrared image from NASA's Cassini spacecraft.

DAPHNIS
Daphnis is another moon found within Saturn's rings. As it orbits the planet, the moon's gravity affects the material within the rings, creating wavelike ripples along the edges of the rings.

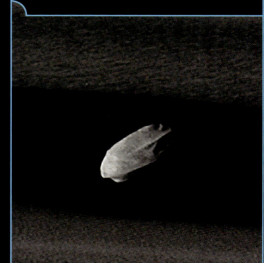

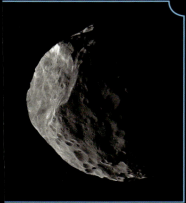

MIMAS
Mimas is the smallest of Saturn's major moons and the closest to the gas giant. Covered in craters, it is home to the enormous Herschel Crater, which measures 87 miles (140 km) wide—so large that scientists are surprised it didn't destroy Mimas.

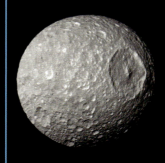

78 • CASSINI-HUYGENS

LAUNCH DATE
October 15, 1997

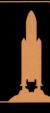

JOURNEY TIME
It took 7 years for Cassini to reach Saturn, utilizing flybys of Venus and Jupiter to boost its journey.

- **2** First Venus flyby
- **3** Second Venus flyby
- **6** Arrival at Saturn
- **CASSINI**
- **1** Launch
- **4** Earth flyby
- **5** Jupiter flyby

SIZE
22 ft (6.7 m long by
13 ft (4 m) wide.

TOP SPEED
98,346 mph (158,273 kph)

WAKE UP CALLS
Cassini-Huygens was put in low-power mode during its journey to Saturn and was reactivated from time to time by NASA to make sure it was still working.

HUYGENS LANDER
In 2005, Huygens landed on Titan—it was the most distant landing ever achieved by a spacecraft from Earth. The Huygens lander operated on Titan for around 3½ hours.

The **Cassini** mission collected **635 GIGABYTES OF DATA**—that's equivalent to 159,000 high-resolution photos.

Cassini's **communication dish** was about 13 ft (4 m) in diameter—it had to be large to beam signals across the colossal distances between Saturn and Earth.

CASSINI'S mission ended in 2017—when fuel ran out, it plunged into **SATURN'S** clouds but it continued to take images until the very end.

Exploring Saturn

CASSINI-HUYGENS WAS ONE OF THE LARGEST SPACECRAFT TO ORBIT ANOTHER PLANET. Over the course of 13 years, it studied Saturn in remarkable detail. Cassini discovered two new rings and identified seven previously unknown moons orbiting the planet. It worked out Saturn's day length—how long it takes to make one full rotation on its axis—and observed the seasonal color changes of the planet's unique hexagonal storm. The spacecraft also carried a small lander named Huygens.

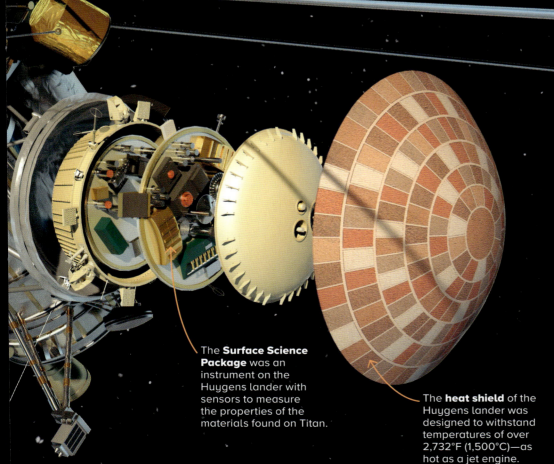

This is one of three long **antennas** used to detect radio waves in Saturn's outer atmosphere.

The **Surface Science Package** was an instrument on the Huygens lander with sensors to measure the properties of the materials found on Titan.

The **heat shield** of the Huygens lander was designed to withstand temperatures of over 2,732°F (1,500°C)—as hot as a jet engine.

HUYGENS ON TITAN

The focus of the Huygens mission was not Saturn but its largest moon, Titan. The lander separated from Cassini, having traveled with it for seven years, and parachuted down to the moon's surface. Huygens discovered lakes of methane and a landscape littered with orange-brown pebbles.

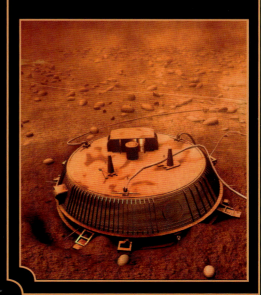

THE CASSINI-HUYGENS mission was an international effort, involving NASA, the European Space Agency, and the Italian Space Agency. It was a complex mission because it involved operating two spacecraft that would eventually separate to carry out their own scientific explorations.

URANUS

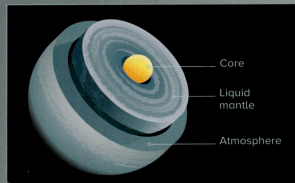

ICE GIANT
Uranus's outer layers are made mostly of hydrogen and helium gas and some methane, which gives the planet its distinctive blue color. But unlike the gas giants Jupiter and Saturn, Uranus's small, dense core is surrounded by an icy layer of water, ammonia, and methane.

Side Spinner

URANUS IS AN EXTRAORDINARY WORLD. It is the only planet in the solar system that orbits the sun on its side. This sideways tilt results in the most extreme seasons of any planet—each pole experiences 42 years of sunlight and 42 years of darkness. Like the other gas giants in the solar system, Uranus has rings.

Uranus is the coldest planet in the solar system.

Uranus's **clouds** have **HYDROGEN SULFIDE**—the same chemical that gives rotten eggs their unpleasant **SMELL**.

Uranus's moon **MIRANDA** has the **tallest cliff** in the solar system—its height is almost **FOUR TIMES** the depth of the Grand Canyon in the US.

Miranda
32,800 ft (10,000 m)

Point Imperial, Grand Canyon
8,802 ft (2,683 m)

URANUS is largely featureless as can be seen in this image taken by NASA's Voyager 2. But massive storms around the planet's north pole and infrared auroras have been detected.

URANUS • 81

Methane in the atmosphere absorbs red and yellow light and reflects blue, giving Uranus its color.

Faint **bands of cloud** are formed from methane and sulfurous gases.

DIAMETER

Earth — 7,926 miles / 12,756 km

Uranus — 31,763 miles / 51,118 km

YEAR

EARTH **365 days**

URANUS **30,688 Earth days**

DAY

Earth — 24 hours

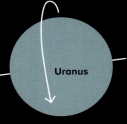

Uranus — 17 hours

CLOUD-TOP TEMPERATURE

-323°F (-197°C)

AURORAS

Uranus's magnetic field tilts about 60° from the axis of its rotation, causing the planet's auroras to be far from the poles.

RINGS AND MOONS

Uranus has a faint set of 13 rings and 28 known moons, which also rotate sideways. The rings are made of dust and are hard to see as they don't reflect much sunlight. This image was taken by the James Webb Space Telescope, which captured the ring system, moons (blue dots), and the north polar ice cap.

Moon · Ice cap

82 • NEPTUNE

SIZE

Earth — 7,926 miles / 12,756 km
Neptune — 30,775 miles / 49,528 km

YEAR
EARTH 365 days
NEPTUNE 60,190 Earth days

DAY

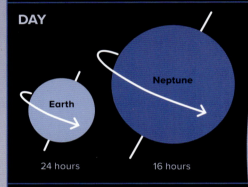

Earth — 24 hours
Neptune — 16 hours

CLOUD-TOP TEMPERATURE
-330°F (-201°C)

MOONS

So far 16 moons have been found orbiting Neptune. Only one of them, Triton, is spherical.

Triton, Proteus, Larissa, Galatea, Despina, Naiad

GOLDEN RECORD

Launched in 1977, NASA's Voyager 2 probe took 12 years to reach Neptune. On its marathon mission, it carried a golden disk engraved with music, greetings in 55 languages, images, and sounds from Earth.

The wisps and bands of cloud seen on Neptune are whisked around the planet by some of the **fastest winds** in the solar system.

NEPTUNE'S colossal storm, the Great Dark Spot, was captured by NASA's Voyager 2 in 1989. It was the first spacecraft to observe the planet.

NEPTUNE • 83

The **Great Dark Spot** was a storm the size of Earth. It had vanished by 1994.

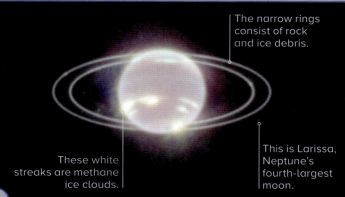

The narrow rings consist of rock and ice debris.

These white streaks are methane ice clouds.

This is Larissa, Neptune's fourth-largest moon.

DUSTY RINGS
NASA's James Webb Space Telescope captured this spectacular infrared image of Neptune and its faint, dusty rings. The five rings appear to be shrinking, and some scientists think they will start disappearing in the next 100 years.

Ice Giant

NEPTUNE IS THE MOST DISTANT PLANET IN OUR SOLAR SYSTEM. It is also the most recently discovered planet. In 1846, having made some calculations, astronomers pointed their telescopes to where they thought it would be—they had found the eighth planet of the solar system. Neptune is made mostly of icy ammonia, water, and methane around a small, rocky core. The planet, which gets its striking blue color from sunlight shining on the methane, is surrounded by faint rings.

Neptune's largest moon Triton is slowly falling toward the planet and in about **3.6 BILLION YEARS** Neptune's gravity will tear it apart.

Neptune's **WIND SPEEDS** can reach more than **1,240 MPH (2,000 kph)**— the strongest and fastest of any planet in the solar system.

84 • PLUTO

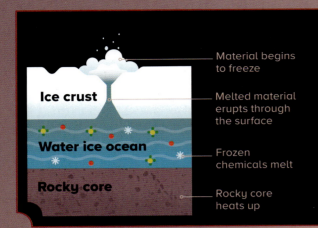

ICE VOLCANOES

Two massive, unusual-looking mountains that may be cryovolcanoes have been discovered on Pluto. Instead of erupting molten rock like the volcanoes on Earth, a slushy mix of liquids and ice flows to the surface and then freezes. Scientists believe this activity is driven by heat generated from decaying radioactive elements in Pluto's rocky core.

Small World

PLUTO USED TO BE DESCRIBED AS THE NINTH PLANET IN THE SOLAR SYSTEM. In 2006, however, it was reclassified as a dwarf planet due to its small size. Pluto orbits the sun far out in the solar system—it took NASA's New Horizons spacecraft just over nine years to reach the dwarf planet, arriving in 2015. The spacecraft sent back images revealing mountains, canyons, volcanoes, and a massive, heart-shaped ice region.

Like the **BUBBLES** of a lava lamp, new ice bubbles move up to replace the old ice on **PLUTO'S SURFACE.**

The compounds present on Pluto's surface give rise to **rich colors**, from deep black to bright red areas.

Pluto — 5½ hours

It takes **SUNLIGHT 5½ HOURS** to reach Pluto.

Earth — 8 minutes

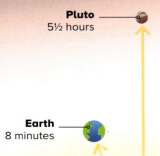

PLUTO'S surface colors have been enhanced in this image taken by NASA's New Horizons spacecraft. Each land feature has its own color, revealing its chemical composition.

PLUTO • 85

The **heart-shaped** region is called Tombaugh Regio—named in honor of American astronomer Clyde Tombaugh, who discovered Pluto in 1930.

Wright Mons, named after the American aviation pioneers the Wright brothers, may be a cryovolcano.

SIZE

Earth — 7,926 miles / 12,756 km
Pluto — 1,476 miles / 2,376 km

YEAR

EARTH **365 days**
PLUTO **90,560 Earth days**

DAY

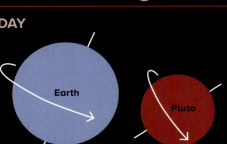

Earth 24 hours
Pluto 153 hours

SURFACE TEMPERATURE

-387°F (-233°C)

MOONS

Pluto has five moons. The largest of these is Charon, which is half the size of Pluto.

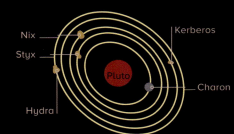

Nix, Styx, Hydra, Kerberos, Charon, Pluto

ATMOSPHERE

Pluto has an extremely thin atmosphere made up of nitrogen and methane. It is 100,000 times thinner than Earth's atmosphere.

Methane / Nitrogen

86 • COMETS

Space Snowballs

SOMETIMES A COMET CROSSES THE NIGHT SKY BEFORE DISAPPEARING BACK INTO SPACE. Comets are made of ice, gases, and dust left over from the formation of the solar system. Occasionally, these visitors from outer space are knocked into new orbits by the gravity of nearby planets or other space objects, bringing them into the inner solar system. As they approach the sun, the ice on their surface evaporates, releasing gas and dust, which form two separate tails that glow in the night sky.

Escaping gases and dust form an atmosphere around the comet known as a **coma**.

The frozen core of a comet is called the **nucleus**—it is also known as a dirty snowball.

COMET LEONARD, shown here, was first spotted in January 2021. It made its closest approach to Earth in December 2021, blazing across the night sky. It will not be visible from Earth again as its orbit takes it away from the sun and into the outer solar system forever.

SIZE

A comet's nucleus can range in size from a few yards to tens of miles across. Its tail can be over

600,000 miles
(1 million km) long.

LOCATION

Scientists estimate that there are about 12 trillion comets in the Oort Cloud—a massive spherical cloud surrounding the solar system. Comets are also found in the Kuiper Belt, which lies beyond the orbit of Neptune.

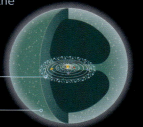

Kuiper Belt

Oort Cloud

solar system

TYPES OF COMET

There are two types of comet:

Long-period comets come from the Oort Cloud and take more than 200 years to orbit the Sun.

Short-period comets come from the Kuiper Belt and take less than 200 years to orbit the Sun.

Long-period comet

COMETS 87

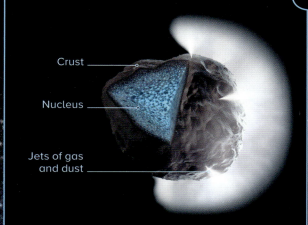

COMET'S NUCLEUS

The nucleus of a comet is made up of a mix of dust and ice held together by gravity. Its surface is covered by a layer of dark carbon compounds that absorb most of the sunlight, making comet nuclei some of the darkest objects in the solar system. On the side facing the sun, jets of gas and dust erupt as the sun's warmth causes the surface to evaporate.

Dust and gas released from the coma get blown away by the solar wind and radiation, creating two tails—a gas tail (blue) and a dust tail (white).

The word "**comet**" comes from the Greek word *kometes*, meaning **LONG-HAIRED STAR.**

Short-period comet

MEGA COMET

The biggest comet discovered so far—Comet Bernardinelli-Bernstein—is about

80 miles (129 km)

across and weighs over

500 trillion tons

(450 trillion tonnes).

It was originally mistaken for a dwarf planet.

GREEN COMA

The Green Comet was first spotted in California, US, in 2022. It was last visible from Earth around 50,000 years ago, during the Stone Age. Its distinctive green coma is due to gases such as carbon and cyanogen, which emit green light when exposed to sunlight.

LAUNCH DATE

March 2, 2004

FLYBYS

To reach 67P/Churyumov-Gerasimenko, Rosetta made three flybys of Earth and one of Mars.

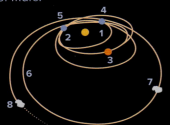

1. Earth departure
2. First Earth flyby
3. Mars flyby
4. Second Earth flyby
5. Third Earth flyby
6. Entry into deep space
7. Arrival at comet
8. Mission end on comet

SPACECRAFT SIZE

ROSETTA

9 ft m
(2.8 m)
(without solar panels)

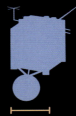

PHILAE

3.3 ft
(1 m) wide

COMET SIZE

2.7 miles
(4.3 km) long

MISSION END

Rosetta orbited the comet for 2 years. The mission ended in September 2016 when the spacecraft made a planned crash-landing, joining Philae on the comet's surface.

SPACE TOOLS

The lander was equipped with tools to analyze gases and surface materials. It also beamed radio signals through the comet to find out more about its internal structure.

Comet Chaser

IN 2014, THE SPACE PROBE ROSETTA REACHED ITS DESTINATION IN THE OUTER SOLAR SYSTEM—comet 67P/Churyumov-Gerasimenko. The journey, which took a decade, required Rosetta to use the gravity of Earth and Mars to get enough speed, like a slingshot maneuver through space, before it reached its target. This mission marked the first time a spacecraft had successfully reached a comet. Equipped with cameras, Rosetta mapped the surface of the comet. It also released the lander Philae.

Philae was the **FIRST CRAFT** to land on a **COMET.**

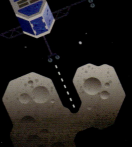

THE ROSETTA ORBITER flew by two asteroids, gathering information on them before reaching the comet, where it released the Philae lander, as shown in this illustration.

ROSETTA AND PHILAE · 89

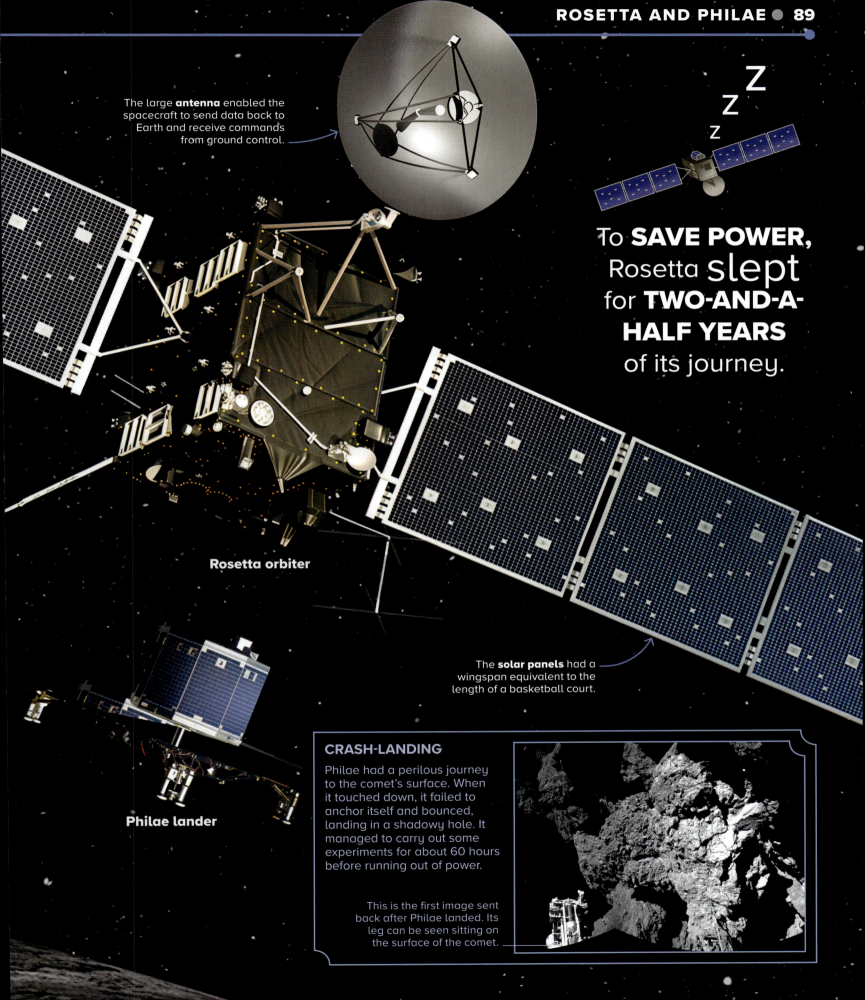

The large **antenna** enabled the spacecraft to send data back to Earth and receive commands from ground control.

To **SAVE POWER**, Rosetta slept for **TWO-AND-A-HALF YEARS** of its journey.

Rosetta orbiter

The **solar panels** had a wingspan equivalent to the length of a basketball court.

Philae lander

CRASH-LANDING

Philae had a perilous journey to the comet's surface. When it touched down, it failed to anchor itself and bounced, landing in a shadowy hole. It managed to carry out some experiments for about 60 hours before running out of power.

This is the first image sent back after Philae landed. Its leg can be seen sitting on the surface of the comet.

90 ● NEW HORIZONS

PLUTO'S ICY HEART

Before New Horizons reached Pluto, the only images we had of the dwarf planet were blurry. New Horizons unlocked the mystery of Pluto's surface and revealed a vast, pale heart-shaped area. The left side of the heart, named Sputnik Planitia, is believed to be the site of an impact. The right side of the heart is a layer of nitrogen ice that has blown across from the left side.

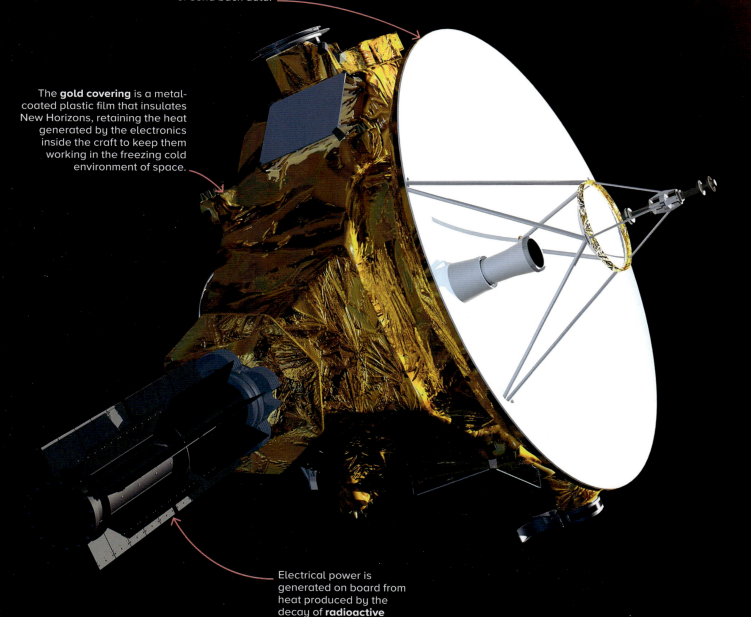

New Horizons's dish-shaped **antenna** is 6.9 ft (2.1 m) across. Given the spacecraft's distance, it takes more than four hours to receive commands from Earth or send back data.

The **gold covering** is a metal-coated plastic film that insulates New Horizons, retaining the heat generated by the electronics inside the craft to keep them working in the freezing cold environment of space.

Electrical power is generated on board from heat produced by the decay of **radioactive plutonium**.

Mission to Pluto

New Horizons flew within 7,800 miles (12,500 km) of Pluto in 2015. When the spacecraft made its flyby, it was about 3 billion miles (5 billion km) from Earth.

NASA'S NEW HORIZONS IS THE FIRST SPACECRAFT SENT TO PLUTO. Launched in 2006, it flew by Jupiter the following year, using the planet's gravity to accelerate its journey. Nearly a decade after its launch, New Horizons reached Pluto, providing the first close-up views of the dwarf planet and its moons. The mission continues as the spacecraft explores the Kuiper Belt in the outer solar system, sending back valuable scientific data.

The amount of **DATA** collected by New Horizons took **16** months to transmit back to Earth.

NEW HORIZONS can reach speeds more than **60** times faster than a **JETLINER.**

LAUNCH DATE
January 19, 2006

DISTANCE COVERED
3 billion miles (5 billion km) to Pluto

VOLCANIC MOON

The spacecraft witnessed massive volcanic eruption on Io, Jupiter's third-largest moon and the most volcanically active object in our solar system.

FIVE MOONS

New Horizons studied Pluto's five moons, revealing the detailed surface of the largest moon, Charon. It also discovered that the four much smaller outer moons spin wildly as they orbit Pluto.

SPACE SNOWMAN

In 2019, New Horizons flew by Arrokoth in the Kuiper Belt. This celestial body was formed from the merger of two icy objects, resulting in a "snowman" appearance. Arrokoth is the most distant object ever explored by a spacecraft.

MICROCHIP

New Horizons was controlled by the same processing chip as the Sony Playstation. This had to be specially adapted to protect it from harmful space radiation.

Home Galaxy

THE MILKY WAY, OUR HOME GALAXY, FORMED ABOUT 13 BILLION YEARS AGO. It is a vast collection of stars, gas, and dust as well as the planets of the solar system. At the heart of the Milky Way is a supermassive black hole known as Sagittarius A*, which contains the mass of 4.3 million suns and swallows anything that ventures near it.

It takes our sun and the solar system **230 MILLION YEARS** to complete **ONE ORBIT** around the center of the **Milky Way.**

Giant **bubbles** of hot gas, known as **FERMI BUBBLES,** hover over the **MILKY WAY,** generating energy equivalent to thousands of exploding stars.

SIZE
The Milky Way is **88,000 light years** in diameter. This means that if you could travel at the speed of light, it would take you 88,000 years to travel from one end to the other.

SIDE-ON VIEW
Seen from the side, the Milky Way has a central bulge. This region is densely packed with the galaxy's oldest stars. The flat disk surrounding the central area is full of young blue and white stars that make up the swirling arms.

Sun · Flat disk · Galactic center · Star cluster

COSMIC COLLISION
Data collected from ESA's Gaia spacecraft indicates that about 10 billion years ago, the Milky Way either collided or merged with a smaller galaxy, creating the structure of our home galaxy that we see today.

GALACTIC ESCAPE
If you could travel at 1 million mph (1.6 million kph) you would break free of the Milky Way's gravity and be able to visit another galaxy.

UNUSUAL CHEMICAL
Scientists have found a chemical called ethyl formate in the center of our galaxy. This chemical gives raspberries their smell and taste.

SPIRAL GALAXY
The Milky Way is a spiral galaxy. Our sun and the planets of the solar system lie in one of its arms, called the Orion Spur. A dark halo surrounds the galaxy. Now known to be dark matter, the halo acts like a cosmic "glue," keeping the Milky Way together.

Galactic center · Orion Spur · dark matter · black hole · solar system

MILKY WAY • 93

Everything in the galaxy orbits **Sagittarius A*** at the heart of the galactic center.

New stars form within the vast clouds of **dust and gas**, which are bigger than our solar system.

THE MILKY WAY is just one of billions of galaxies in the Universe. It is estimated to contain between 100 billion and 400 billion stars, including our sun. From studying the position of stars, scientists created this image of what we think the Milky Way looks like.

Glowing Arc
All the **stars** you see in the night sky are in our galaxy. But from Earth, we can only see part of the **Milky Way**—the edge of the galaxy's disk arching across the sky. This glowing arc is created by the light of billions of stars. The dark patches within the arc are clouds of dust and gas that block the light of other stars.

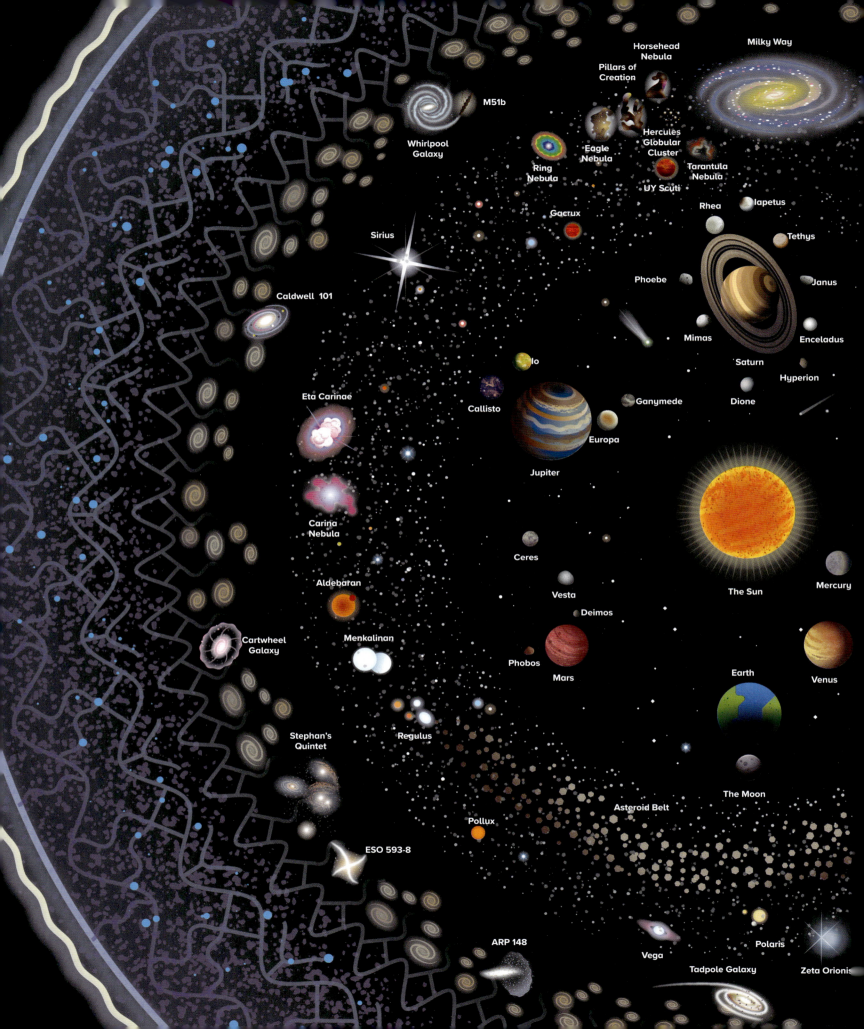

Looking at the Universe

The solar system is part of the Milky Way, a galaxy containing at least 100 billion stars. Our home galaxy is just one of countless galaxies in the universe. Ultra-powerful telescopes can see billions of light years into outer space, revealing never-before-seen stars, nebulas, and galaxies.

98 ● DEEP FIELD

The light from **very distant galaxies**, such as this elliptical one, appears red.

The light from **closer galaxies**, such as this spiral one, appears white.

Nearby stars are so bright that their light creates an **eight-point pattern**, which is due to the hexagonal design of the JWST's mirror.

This central, bright **cluster of galaxies** is SMACS 0723.

THE JWST'S DEEP FIELD image shows ancient galaxies that formed between 500 and 700 million years after the Big Bang. It is the most distant, detailed infrared view of the universe to date.

DEEP FIELD • 99

Distant Universe

THIS IMAGE OF THE EARLY UNIVERSE IS KNOWN AS A DEEP FIELD. It was taken by the James Webb Space Telescope (JWST) in 2022. By focusing on an area of space no bigger than a pinhead to our eyes, the telescope provided the most distant and detailed infrared view of the universe to date. At the center of this breathtaking image is the galaxy cluster SMACS 0723, seen as it was 4.6 billion years ago.

Some of the galaxies in this **DEEP FIELD** image appear as they were 13 billion years ago, shortly after the Big Bang.

About **95** percent of the **UNIVERSE** is invisible—made up of **DARK MATTER** and **DARK ENERGY**.

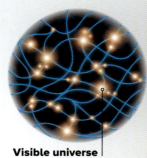
Visible universe

BIG BANG
About 13.8 billion years ago, the universe expanded suddenly from a single point. This beginning is called the Big Bang. The universe is still expanding today.

LOCATION
The galaxy cluster SMACS 0723 is located in the southern constellation Volans (the Flying Fish). Although we see it as it was 4.6 billion years ago, the cluster itself is much older.

SMACS 0723

COSMIC TIME
When you look at stars in the night sky, you are looking back in time. That's because light from these stars has taken years to reach us on Earth.

MAGNIFYING GLASS
Galaxy clusters such as SMACS 0723 have so much mass and gravity that they warp spacetime. This causes light from a galaxy behind the cluster to bend around it, magnifying the image and letting the JWST see even further back in time.

ANCIENT GALAXIES
The ancient galaxies look more like clumps than the well-defined spirals and elliptical galaxies we see today.

SNAPSHOT
The JWST photographed the ancient universe, with some galaxies as they were 13 billion years ago, in 12½ hours. That's a fraction compared to the 10 days that the Hubble Space Telescope took for its first Deep Field image in 1995.

Brown Dwarf

The James Webb Space Telescope (JWST) is able to observe objects in infrared, and this has led to the discovery of new brown dwarfs. These are objects that emit most of their radiation in infrared and are too big to be planets but not massive enough to be stars. This artist's impression of a brown dwarf with an aurora is based on a brown dwarf spotted by the JWST.

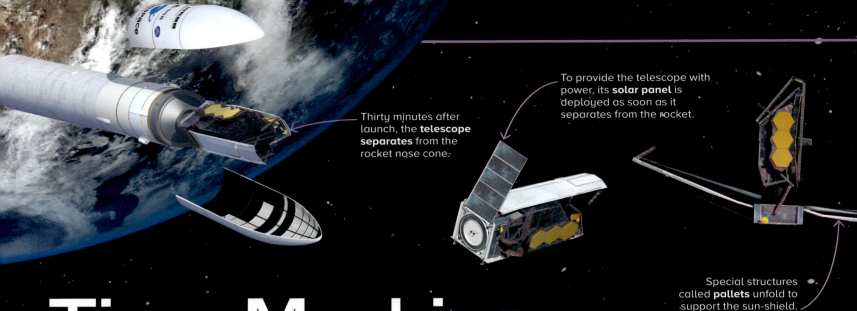

Thirty minutes after launch, the **telescope separates** from the rocket nose cone.

To provide the telescope with power, its **solar panel** is deployed as soon as it separates from the rocket.

Special structures called **pallets** unfold to support the sun-shield.

Time Machine

THE JAMES WEBB SPACE TELESCOPE (JWST) IS AN INCREDIBLE FEAT OF ENGINEERING. Standing as tall as a three-story building and as wide as a tennis court, it had to fit into its launch rocket, Ariane 5, which is only 17.7 ft (5.4 m) in diameter. To achieve this, it was designed to fold into twelve segments and unfurl in space. Now, the world's most powerful space telescope is peering into space, providing scientists with views of the distant universe never seen before.

THE JAMES WEBB SPACE TELESCOPE took 13 days to unfold in space, as shown in these artist's illustrations. NASA had identified 344 possible points of failure, but the entire process worked perfectly.

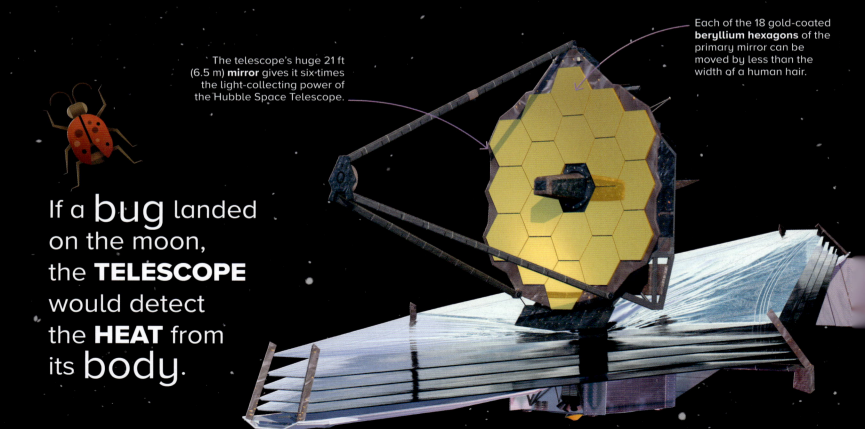

The telescope's huge 21 ft (6.5 m) **mirror** gives it six times the light-collecting power of the Hubble Space Telescope.

Each of the 18 gold-coated **beryllium hexagons** of the primary mirror can be moved by less than the width of a human hair.

If a **bug** landed on the moon, the **TELESCOPE** would detect the **HEAT** from its **body**.

JAMES WEBB SPACE TELESCOPE

A set of extendable arms called **booms** drag out the five-layer sun-shield.

Microshutters allow the telescope to observe **100 different objects** in space at the same time.

Three arms arranged as a tripod flip down to support a smaller **secondary mirror**.

The two side wings of the **primary mirror** flip out to complete the telescope.

HOW IT WORKS

The JWST looks for infrared light—light that has been stretched out from distant early stars. Infrared light can pass through gas and dust across the vast expanse of space, allowing us to see objects that are otherwise invisible.

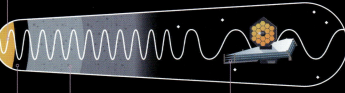

Big Bang • Dark ages before stars • First stars • The expanding universe stretches the light of the first stars into infrared light.

LAUNCH DATE
December 25, 2021

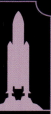

MISSION DURATION
up to **20 years**

LOCATION
The JWST orbits the sun at a location known as the second Lagrange point (L2)—930,000 miles (1.5 million km) from Earth. The telescope's sun-shield protects it from the sun's heat.

L2 • Earth • moon • sun

EARLY GALAXY
The telescope has captured the most distant known galaxy—called JADES-GS-z14-0—as it was about 290 million years after the Big Bang.

SUNBLOCK
The JWST's five-layer sun-shield is like a sunblock with a sun protection factor of 1 million. The sun-shield prevents the telescope's instruments from overheating.

GOLDEN MIRROR
The JWST's massive mirrors are coated with a very thin layer of gold, which is used to reflect light. If you scraped off the gold, it would weigh about the same as a golf ball.

103

Space Origami
The **James Webb Space Telescope**, including its **colossal primary mirror**, was tested extensively before its launch. The hexagonal sections had to align perfectly. They also needed to fold origami-style so that they could fit inside the rocket and then unfold correctly once the space telescope reached its destination.

106 • AMAZING SPACE

TARANTULA
Inside the giant Tarantula Nebula, the JWST captured not just the bright, blue stars at the center, but tens of thousands of reddish stars, still surrounded by the dust from which they are forming.

The long wavelength of **INFRARED LIGHT** allows it to pass through dust clouds that block visible light.

CARTWHEEL GALAXY
The unusual ring shape of the Cartwheel Galaxy is the result of a high-speed cosmic collision between two galaxies. The JWST's sensitive cameras have revealed details of the supernovas and star formation triggered by the chaos.

SERPENS
Peering into the Serpens Nebula is like looking back in time to the first few million years of our own solar system. At its center are sunlike stars, surrounded by disks of debris that will one day form planets.

AMAZING SPACE • 107

NGC 604
Located in the Triangulum Galaxy, the nebula NGC 604 is 2.73 million light years from Earth. The JWST found an unusual collection of super-hot stars—each up to 100 times more massive than our sun—inside the nebula.

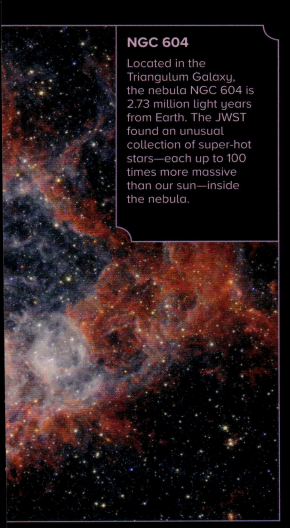

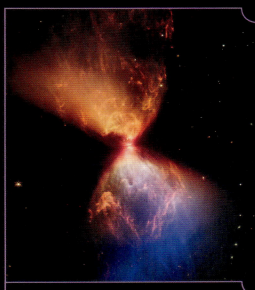

PROTOSTAR L1527
Inside the dark dust cloud L1527, the JWST detected a protostar (newly forming star). The baby star feeds on the dust and burps out jets of gas that glow as they collide with the surrounding stardust.

STAR CLUSTER IC 348
This image from the JWST shows the star cluster IC 348. Although brown dwarfs are far larger than planets, these stars did not gather enough mass to ignite. This makes them very difficult to detect. However, the JWST spotted three brown dwarfs within this star cluster.

CASSIOPEIA A
Supernovas are briefly the brightest objects in the night sky. To the sensors of the JWST, their blast clouds are just as spectacular. The supernova remnant Cassiopeia A, about 11,000 light years from Earth, reveals information about the past and future of the dead star.

Amazing Space

DUSTY AREAS OF SPACE WERE SOME OF THE FIRST TARGETS FOR THE JAMES WEBB SPACE TELESCOPE (JWST). These star nurseries, galaxies, and supernova-blast clouds had already been photographed by telescopes such as Hubble, but the JWST offers the chance to peer through the dust that blocks visible light, to reveal previously hidden details.

The **JAMES WEBB SPACE TELESCOPE** can detect objects that glow **540,000 TIMES** more faintly than those we can detect with our eyes.

ETA CARINAE

LOCATION
Eta Carinae lies in the southern constellation Carina (the Keel).

SIZE
The main star is estimated to be about 100 times bigger than the sun, while the smaller star is about 40 times the size of the sun.

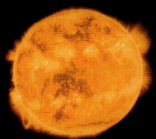

DISTANCE FROM EARTH
7,500 light years

ORBIT
The stars orbit around each other, taking **5½ years** to make a full circuit.

LASER BEAM
The Hubble Space Telescope detected an ultraviolet laser beam radiating from Eta Carinae. This is the only known instance of a star producing such an emission.

STAR DEATH
No one knows when Eta Carinae A will explode. It may even explode as a hypernova, which is 10 to 100 million times more explosive than a supernova. When it does explode, it will light our skies both day and night.

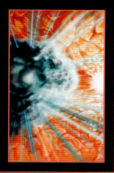

Time Bomb

ETA CARINAE IS A STAR SYSTEM MADE UP OF TWO MASSIVE STARS. Together, the stars are among the most luminous in the Milky Way. They are surrounded by a billowing dumbbell-shaped cloud of gas and dust, called the Homunculus Nebula. The larger of the stars is expected to explode in a supernova—one of the biggest types of explosion in the universe. The turbulent stars hurl a colossal amount of gas and dust into space—enough to cover the entire solar system.

Eta Carinae is about **5 MILLION TIMES** more luminous than the sun.

The lobes of **gas and dust** that surround the monster stars move through space at more than **1.2 MILLION MPH** (2 million kph).

CARINA NEBULA
The Homunculus Nebula is located within the Carina Nebula—one of the most active regions of star birth and death. The Carina Nebula is home to many young stars that are much larger than our sun. Intense stellar winds and radiation sculpt the nebula's appearance, while the clouds of gas are illuminated by the energy of newborn stars.

ETA CARINAE 109

The **larger star** will eventually run out of fuel and **explode.**

The **fainter outer shell** of gas and dust is evidence of a much earlier explosion.

ETA CARINAE experienced a cataclysmic explosion, which was spotted in 1837, ejecting material that created the lobes of gas and dust seen in this image taken by the Hubble Space Telescope.

V838 MONOCEROTIS

LOCATION
V838 Monocerotis is in the constellation Monoceros (the Unicorn).

V838 Monocerotis

DISTANCE FROM EARTH
20,000 light years from Earth, on the outer edge of the Milky Way

SIZE
The red supergiant is almost 500 times as wide as our sun. The surrounding nebula is more than **7 light years** across.

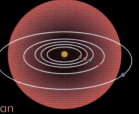

LUMINOSITY
About **23,000 times** as bright as our sun

DISCOVERY
Astronomers were alerted to the initial brightening in 2002 by an amateur stargazer. They pointed the Hubble Space Telescope at V838 Monocerotis with spectacular results.

Light Echo

A BURST OF LIGHT REVEALED THE SPECTACULAR NEBULA SURROUNDING AN UNUSUAL STAR. V838 Monocerotis captured the world's attention in 2002 when it suddenly became incredibly bright. The initial light burst lasted just three months. However, for years afterward scattered light from the outburst illuminated vast clouds of dust around the star—giving us the chance to see a feature of space that is normally hidden.

During the initial light burst, **V838 MONOCEROTIS** became **600,000** times brighter than **THE SUN**.

The **"ECHO"** of scattered light from the outburst lasted more than **two years**.

STARBURST STAGES
The Hubble Space Telescope tracked V838 Monocerotis's light echo over many months. As it spread out, the echo revealed different parts of the dust shell. The dust also seemed to change color, as the temperature, brightness, and color of V838 Monocerotis changed.

May 2002

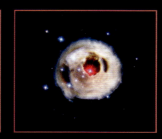
September 2002

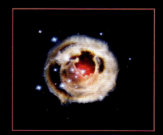
October 2002

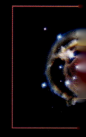
December 2002

V838 MONOCEROTIS • 111

- V838 Monocerotis was already surrounded by a **shell of dust**, which was gradually revealed by the scattered light.

- The type of light burst that V838 Monocerotis went through is called a **red nova**, possibly caused by a collision with another star.

- More distant regions of space are visible through holes in the shell of dust, so this is classified as a **"Swiss cheese"** nebula.

THE HUBBLE SPACE TELESCOPE took this image of the light echo in October 2004, almost three years after the star at its heart, V838 Monocerotis, suddenly brightened.

February 2004

112 ● RHO OPHIUCHI

The **densest area of gas and dust** forms a dark shadow on the image and hides the newly forming star or stars inside.

The bright star S1 releases **stellar winds that push away** the surrounding gas and dust.

Jets of hydrogen burst out in opposite directions from newly forming stars.

THIS IMAGE OF RHO OPHIUCHI was created using several different photographs taken by the James Webb Space Telescope (JWST) to celebrate the telescope's first birthday.

Multicolored Clouds

THIS TINY AREA OF THE MILKY WAY, KNOWN AS RHO OPHIUCHI, REVEALS A SPECTACULAR SCENE AROUND NEWLY FORMING STARS. Most stars in this image are the same size as—or smaller than—our sun. Each one swallows gas and dust around it, while spitting out jets of hydrogen that disturb the surrounding area. Only when a star has found the right balance does it become stable and begin to clear the space around it with a steady stellar wind.

Around **50 STARS** lie in the **area of space** captured by this image.

The surrounding **RHO OPHIUCHI** cloud complex contains enough **GAS** and **DUST** to form **3,000 suns**.

Newly forming sunlike star

COLORFUL CLOUDS
This small, dark area of space in the JWST's image is surrounded by a much bigger area of cotton candy-colored clouds, known as the Rho Ophiuchi cloud complex. Because this area is so close to Earth, it looks huge in the night sky.

Seen from Earth — **Cloud complex** — **JWST detail**

LOCATION
The Rho Ophiuchi cloud complex lies across the constellations Scorpius (the Scorpion) and Ophiuchus (the Serpent Bearer).

Rho Opiuchi

DISTANCE FROM EARTH
The Rho Ophiuchi cloud complex lies just

390 light years

from Earth in the Milky Way, making it our nearest star-forming region.

SUPER-COLD CLOUDS
Although they are lit by the surrounding stars, the clouds themselves are very cold.

COLOR CHANGES
The blue areas of the Rho Ophiuchu cloud complex are created by starlight bouncing off dust particles. The red areas are caused by hydrogen gas that glows when it is energized by ultraviolet light from hot young stars.

SUNLIKE STARS
Because this region contains so many sun-sized stars, it gives us a glimpse of what our own cosmic neighborhood looked like almost

5 billion years ago.

FLYING SAUCER
In 2001, a young star surrounded by a ring-shaped disk of gas and dust was discovered in the Rho Ophiuchi star-forming region. Nicknamed the "Flying Saucer," it provides scientists with important information as to how stars and planets form.

Star Nursery

THE MAGNIFICENT PILLARS OF CREATION IN THE EAGLE NEBULA ARE PACKED WITH NEWBORN STARS. Jutting into space like ghostly fingers, these vast columns of gas and dust amazed the world when first photographed by the Hubble space Telescope in 1995. Although these columns are sites of star formation, they are slowly being destroyed by the very stars they help create—but not before the James Webb space Telescope's infrared cameras revealed a host of new details.

LOCATION
The Pillars of Creation are a small part of the vast Eagle Nebula (M16) located in the Northern Hemisphere constellation of serpens, which represents a snake.

Pillars of Creation

SIZE
Our entire solar system would fit in the **"fingertip"** of just one pillar.

DISTANCE FROM EARTH
The Eagle Nebula lies within the Milky Way galaxy and is **6,500 light years** from Earth.

AGE
5½ million years old, the nebula is relatively young compared to other celestial objects. For example, our sun is 4.6 billion years old.

INVISIBLE DETAILS
Our eyes can't see infrared light, so software is used to translate data collected by the JWST's near-infrared camera into visible-light images.

STAR LIFE
The stars in the Pillars of Creation are estimated to be between 1 and 10 million years old. Compared to the lifespan of stars, this is a relatively short period as many stars can live for billions of years.

Although they look almost **SOLID,** the gas and dust that make up the pillars are **10 million billion** times **LESS DENSE** than Earth's air.

Gas and dust in the Pillars of Creation

Air on Earth

MAGNETIC FIELD
The Pillars of Creation may keep their shape thanks to their unusual magnetic field. Every particle of gas and dust acts like a tiny compass, lining up with the local magnetic field. Scientists have discovered that the magnetic field inside each column is at right angles to the field outside it. This may stop the hot, charged plasma all around from pressing in and breaking up the column-shaped clouds.

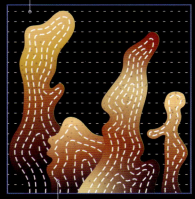

Magnetic field outside the pillars

Magnetic field inside the pillars

PILLARS OF CREATION • 115

Dense **knots of matter** begin to collapse under their own gravity. As they draw together they also heat up, eventually igniting as new stars.

A nebula is a huge cloud of interstellar **hydrogen gas and dust** where many new stars form. The darkest areas are the most dense.

Where the **dust** is cooler and more spread out, it seems to disappear altogether.

The **pillars** are slowly being eroded by light and particles streaming from bright nearby stars.

THE JAMES WEBB SPACE TELESCOPE (JWST) uses a camera that detects infrared energy rather than visible light. This allows the JWST to peer through the dust and gas clouds, revealing thousands of newly forming stars.

Starscape
This stunning image of the **Eagle Nebula** was taken at the La Silla Observatory in Chile. The **Pillars of Creation** can be seen in the center, illuminated by thousands of massive young stars—these stars release powerful ultraviolet light that causes the surrounding gas to glow. But the radiation from the stars is also eroding the pillars, dispersing the gas and dust and triggering further star formation.

118 ● HUBBLE TELESCOPE

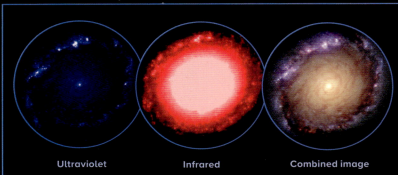

HUBBLE'S IMAGES

As well as visible light, Hubble detects ultraviolet and small amounts of infrared light, which reveals objects whose visible light is obscured by dust. This information is then combined to produce the final image. Shown here is Hubble's view of NGC 1512, a spiral galaxy that is about 30 million light years from Earth.

Ultraviolet | Infrared | Combined image

Hubble in Space

THE HUBBLE SPACE TELESCOPE HAS REWRITTEN OUR UNDERSTANDING OF THE COSMOS. The world's first large space telescope has helped work out the age of the universe and confirm the theory that the universe is expanding. Hubble has also confirmed the existence of supermassive black holes at the heart of galaxies and has found the smallest exoplanet with water in its atmosphere.

The primary mirror inside the telescope collects about **40,000** times more light than the human eye.

ASTRONAUTS ON BOARD THE SPACE SHUTTLE have repaired the Hubble Space Telescope on five separate missions, with the last repair carried out in 2009 before the Space Shuttle was retired. These repairs have allowed the telescope to operate beyond its planned 15-year lifetime.

Every week, **HUBBLE** sends back to Earth **15** gigabytes of data—the equivalent of watching **45 TWO-HOUR MOVIES.**

Hubble has made more than **1.6 MILLION** observations since its launch.

These solar panels generate electricity, which is then stored in batteries within the telescope.

This **antenna** transmits data to Earth.

HUBBLE TELESCOPE • 119

LAUNCH DATE
April 24, 1990

LOCATION
Hubble orbits 340 miles (547 km) above Earth's surface, taking 95 minutes to complete an orbit of Earth.

DISTANCE COVERED
5 billion miles
(3 billion km) around Earth since 1990

BLURRY START
Hubble's first images were blurry—the primary mirror had a tiny flaw. This was corrected during a seven-hour spacewalk by astronauts fitting an optical device that worked like a contact lens.

Before   After

LOOKING BACK

In 1995, Hubble observed a tiny patch of the sky, which showed more than 10,000 galaxies. Known as the Hubble Deep Field, it was the first view of the ancient universe.

HUBBLE'S NAME
The Hubble telescope is named in honor of American astronomer Edwin Hubble. He made important discoveries, including proving the existence of other galaxies beyond the Milky Way, when he observed the Andromeda Galaxy.

Andromeda

Space Repairs
Service missions in space have allowed the Hubble Space Telescope to make **groundbreaking discoveries** for far longer than was planned. American astronauts Story Musgrave and Jeffrey Hoffman are shown here standing on the edge of Space Shuttle Endeavour's robotic arm. They are repairing the telescope while it is docked to Endeavour's cargo bay. But with no more Space Shuttle service missions, NASA engineers can now only repair the still-active telescope remotely.

122 • CRAB NEBULA

LOCATION
The Crab Nebula can be seen through a telescope in the constellation Taurus (the Bull).

SIZE
The nebula is around 11 light years across but still expanding rapidly.

DISTANCE FROM EARTH
The pulsar at the center of the Crab Nebula is **6,500 light years** from Earth.

AGE
The Crab Nebula is about **7,500 years old.**

We see the nebula when it was about 1,000 years old, because its light takes about 6,500 years to reach Earth.

NAME
In 1844, Irish astronomer William Parsons observed the nebula and made a drawing of it. Its wispy filaments resembled a crab's legs, which is how the nebula was given its name. The Crab Nebula is also known as M1, NGC 1952, and Taurus A.

EXPANSION
The Crab Nebula expands at almost **620 miles (1,000 km)** per second.

CRAB PULSAR
In 1968, a star was discovered at the center of the Crab Nebula. It is a type of neutron star called a pulsar that formed during the supernova. It is very small, just 12 miles (20 km) across, but incredibly dense, containing more matter than our sun. As it rotates, the pulsar sends out a beam of electromagnetic radiation from each pole. In this image, the pulsar is the bright white dot at the center.

Cosmic Debris

THIS SPECTACULAR NEBULA'S STORY BEGAN ALMOST 1,000 YEARS AGO. In 1054 CE, Chinese and Japanese astronomers spotted a star so bright, it could be seen even in the daytime. They were watching a supernova—the dramatic death of a massive star. The explosion created a vast cloud of glowing gas and dust, now known as the Crab Nebula.

The **PULSAR** at the center of the **Crab Nebula** spins around **30 TIMES EACH SECOND.**

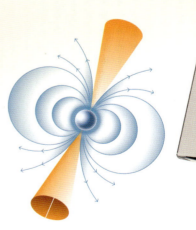

Pulsars send intense **BEAMS OF RADIATION** sweeping across space—from Earth they seem to *flash* like cosmic lighthouses.

CRAB NEBULA ● 123

Grains of stardust still glow with heat from when the star exploded.

Most of the nebula is hydrogen gas, thrown out by the dying star, but **the orange-red areas are made of sulfur.**

IN 2023, NASA'S JAMES WEBB SPACE TELESCOPE captured new details of the Crab Nebula with its powerful infrared instruments. The different components of the nebula can be seen for the first time.

Charged particles zoom around the magnetic field of the pulsar at the center of the nebula, emitting **radiation that glows milky-white** in this image.

124 • HERBIG-HARO 211

LOCATION
HH 211 lies in the constellation Perseus.

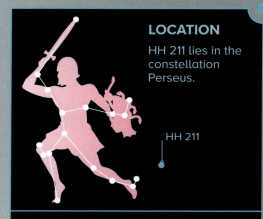

DISTANCE FROM EARTH
HH 211 is about **1,000 light years** from Earth. This makes it one of the nearest young protostar outflows.

AGE
The protostar forming at the centre is known as HH 211-mm. It is thought to be just a few **tens of thousands** of years old.

MASS
So far, the protostar has gathered just 8% of the mass of our sun. Nuclear fusion has not yet begun, so the star is not yet shining.

DIFFERENT WAVELENGTHS
HH 211 has been studied in different wavelengths, including ultraviolet and infrared. Each range of wavelengths shows different details of the HH object.

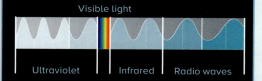

SHOCK WAVES
The pattern of shock waves created by the jets of gas ejected from the protostar suggests the baby star is releasing gas in bursts, as it gobbles up matter from the surrounding nebula.

Baby Stars

SCORCHING NEW SUNS EMERGE FROM COLD CLOUDS OF GAS AND DUST. For the first few millennia, however, those dense clouds hide the newly forming stars, known as protostars. But they make themselves known by the powerful jets of gas that erupt from their poles as they begin to ignite. When the jets collide with gas and dust in space they form glowing "lightsabers" known as Herbig-Haro (HH) objects, such as HH 211, shown here.

The **protostar** at the center of HH 211 is like **OUR OWN SUN** when it was young.

THIS INFRARED IMAGE OF HH 211 was captured by the James Webb Space Telescope (JWST). As superheated gases stream from a young star's poles, they send shock waves rippling through the surrounding nebula.

The **jets of gas** released by the **PROTOSTAR** can move faster than 60 miles (100 km) per second.

HERBIG-HARO 211 • 125

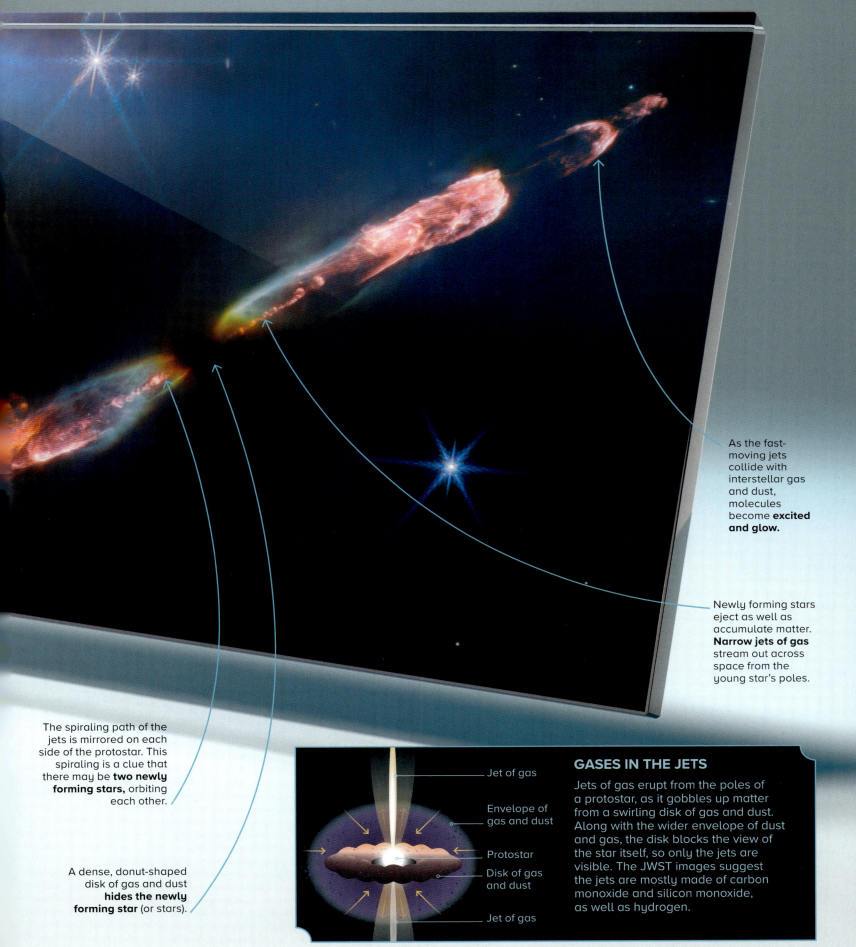

As the fast-moving jets collide with interstellar gas and dust, molecules become **excited and glow.**

Newly forming stars eject as well as accumulate matter. **Narrow jets of gas** stream out across space from the young star's poles.

The spiraling path of the jets is mirrored on each side of the protostar. This spiraling is a clue that there may be **two newly forming stars,** orbiting each other.

A dense, donut-shaped disk of gas and dust **hides the newly forming star** (or stars).

GASES IN THE JETS

Jets of gas erupt from the poles of a protostar, as it gobbles up matter from a swirling disk of gas and dust. Along with the wider envelope of dust and gas, the disk blocks the view of the star itself, so only the jets are visible. The JWST images suggest the jets are mostly made of carbon monoxide and silicon monoxide, as well as hydrogen.

- Jet of gas
- Envelope of gas and dust
- Protostar
- Disk of gas and dust
- Jet of gas

126 • BUBBLE NEBULA

On this side, the stellar wind is moving through cooler, denser gas, so **the bubble has not expanded as far**.

The bright spot reveals the **position of the giant star**, whose powerful radiation and stellar winds have shaped this unusual nebula.

This ridge of dense gas sits outside the bubble. It glows because it has been **energized by intense ultraviolet light** from the star.

THIS IMAGE OF THE BUBBLE NEBULA was created in 2016 using information captured by the Hubble Space Telescope's Wide Field Camera 3 to mark the telescope's 26th birthday. Glowing oxygen is shown in blue, hydrogen in green, and nitrogen in red.

BUBBLE NEBULA ● 127

STELLAR POWERHOUSE
In this wide view, you can see the massive cloud of dense, cool hydrogen, nitrogen, and dust surrounding the Bubble Nebula. The stellar winds push through this cloud, causing the densest areas to glow brightly as they are bathed in the star's strong ultraviolet light.

Hubble's Bubble

THE DELICATE BUBBLE NEBULA IS DESTINED TO POP. Inside the glowing shell is the massive and extremely bright star BD+60°2522. It has burned through its hydrogen fuel and is now fusing helium instead. Fierce stellar winds stream out from the star's surface in all directions, pushing away the cooler cloud of gas that surrounds the star. The outer edges of the bubble reveal where stellar winds meet glowing gas. Such huge stars have short lives, and BD+60°2522 will explode as a supernova in 10 to 20 million years.

BD+60°2522 burns 500,000 times **brighter** than our **SUN**.

The **STELLAR WIND** created by the star travels at over **4 million mph** (6.4 million kph).

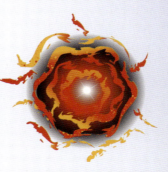

LOCATION
The Bubble Nebula can be seen in the night sky using a telescope pointed toward the constellation Cassiopeia (the Seated Queen).

SIZE
The nebula is about **10 light years** across, but still growing.

DISTANCE FROM EARTH
The Bubble Nebula lies around **8,000 light years** away from Earth, inside our galaxy the Milky Way.

AGE
The star is around **4 million years old,** very young compared to our sun, which has been burning for more than 4 billion years.

EXPANDING BUBBLE
The bubble is expanding at a rate of about **4 miles** (7 km) per second.

DISCOVERY
The Bubble Nebula was discovered in 1787 by German-British astronomer William Herschel. Its official name is NGC 7635.

HERSCHEL'S SELF-BUILT TELESCOPE

128 • HERBIG-HARO 46/47

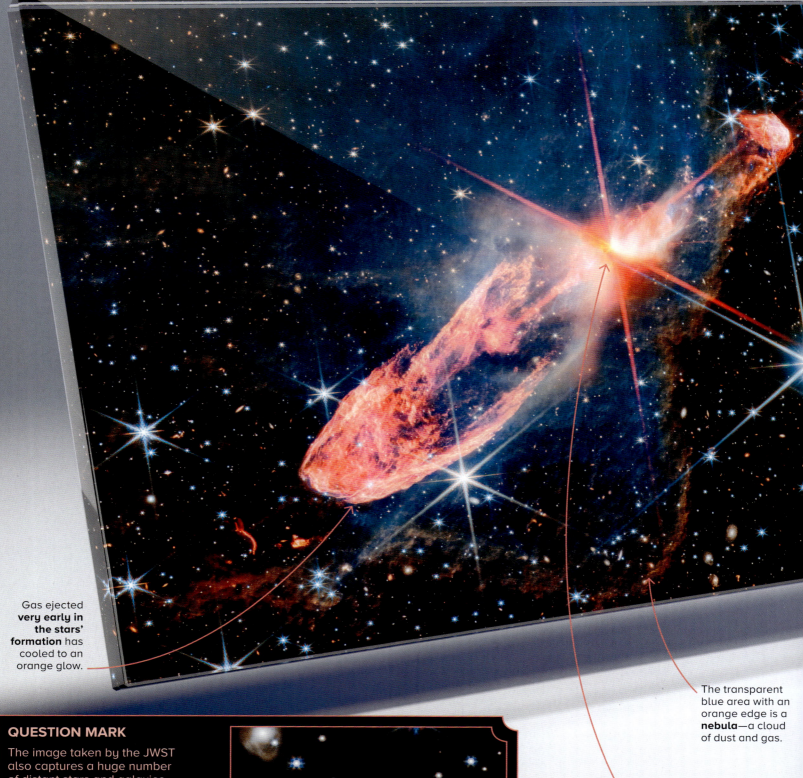

Gas ejected **very early in the stars' formation** has cooled to an orange glow.

The transparent blue area with an orange edge is a **nebula**—a cloud of dust and gas.

The center of the starburst—showing as red due to infrared light bouncing off the telescope's mirror—marks the position of the **two protostars**.

QUESTION MARK

The image taken by the JWST also captures a huge number of distant stars and galaxies lying beyond HH 46/47. One of these glowing objects is particularly intriguing as it looks like a question mark. Its origin remains a mystery, but astronomers think it could be a pair of colliding galaxies.

HERBIG-HARO 46/47 • 129

Although **HH 46/47** glows brightly now, it will one day be **outshone** by the **TWIN STARS**.

The **JETS OF GAS** ejected by the stars travel at speeds of up to **185 MILES** (300 km) **PER SECOND**.

HH46/47 WOULD NOT LOOK like this to our eyes. NASA's James Webb Space Telescope created this image by detecting near-infrared light (heat), and translating it into colors that we can see.

Stellar Twins

A PAIR OF INFANT STARS TIGHTLY BOUND BY GRAVITY IS REVEALED AS THE DUST CLEARS IN A NEWLY FORMING STAR SYSTEM, CALLED HERBIG-HARO 46/47 (HH 46/47). The young stars—known as protostars—have been gobbling up matter from a dusty disk surrounding them. To remain stable, the stars shoot out two huge jets of gas in opposite directions. As the jets collide with dust and gas at high speeds in space, glowing clouds known as Herbig-Haro objects form.

LOCATION
HH 46/47 can be spotted in the constellation Vela (the Sails).

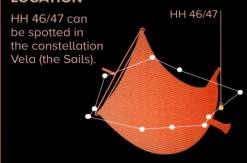

DISTANCE FROM EARTH

1,470 light years

SIZE
The double-sided jet is around

3.1 light years across.

AGE
The protostars are just

a few thousand years old.

They won't be fully formed stars for millions more years.

DISCOVERY
American astronomer Richard D. Schwartz discovered HH 46/47 in 1977, and Dutch-American astronomer Bart Bok was the first to spot its glowing jets, in 1978.

NAME
Herbig-Haro objects are named after American astronomer George Herbig and Mexican astronomer Guillermo Haro, both of whom studied the objects in the 1940s.

Exoplanets

SCIENTISTS SUSPECTED FOR A LONG TIME THAT OUR SUN WAS NOT THE ONLY STAR TO HAVE PLANETS. However, detecting these planets beyond our solar system—known as exoplanets—was difficult, because planets do not glow like stars. But scientists worked out techniques to find them, such as looking for tiny changes in the color or brightness of starlight—clues that a planet is orbiting. Using these techniques, thousands of exoplanets have now been spotted. They are too small and distant to photograph but space agencies have created images to show us what they may look like up close.

ICY GIANTS
As in our own Solar System, temperatures fall the farther a planet is from its star. Beyond a certain point, known as the "snow line," ice giants of a similar mass as Neptune are thought to be common.

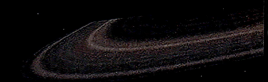

More than **100 BILLION EXOPLANETS** are thought to exist in the **Milky Way**.

HD209458b
This planet orbits just over 4.3 million miles (7 million km) from its Sunlike star—which is actually an uncomfortably close distance. Every second, around 10,000 tons of the planet's gassy atmosphere boils away into space.

WASP-17b
The James Webb Space Telescope detected tiny quartz crystals in the clouds of this massive, Jupiter-like planet, which orbits very close to its star. Scientists think the crystals form due to the intense heat and pressure of the exoplanet's atmosphere.

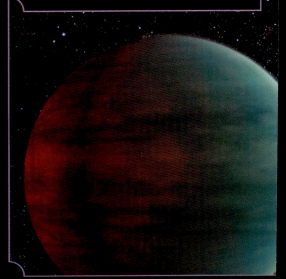

WASP-31b
This planet has around half the mass of Jupiter spread out over a much larger volume. It is less dense than a marshmallow, making it one of the lightest planets spotted so far.

EXOPLANETS • 131

The first exoplanets were **DISCOVERED IN 1992.** More than **5,000** have now been **IDENTIFIED.**

HD189733b
This gas giant is thought to have winds that blow at 5,400 mph (8,690 kph). They whip up blue-toned clouds that rain silicates, which are better known on Earth as glass.

KEPLER 186f
Earth-sized planets in the habitable zone around a star are especially exciting. Such planets are not too hot nor too cold, and they may have life-supporting liquid water on their surface. Kepler 186f was the first exoplanet of this type to be detected.

WASP-19b
More massive than Jupiter, WASP-19b orbits about 60 times closer to its star than Earth does to the Sun. The planet whizzes around its star once every 19 hours—such a fast speed keeps it from falling into the star.

132 • HERCULES GLOBULAR CLUSTER

The **blue-white stars** are far younger and hotter than their neighbors.

The **red and orange stars** are the most ancient, growing in size, cooling, and dimming as they reach the end of their life cycles.

The Hercules Globular Cluster is also known as M13. In this image, created using the Hubble Space Telescope, you can see hundreds of thousands of the individual stars that make up this spectacular cluster.

HERCULES GLOBULAR CLUSTER

Glitter Ball

SOME OF THE OLDEST STARS IN THE UNIVERSE ARE FOUND IN MASSIVE CLUSTERS that orbit large galaxies. The Hercules Globular Cluster contains between 300,000 and 500,000 stars and orbits our own Milky Way. Its stars are held together by their own gravity, creating the ultimate glitter ball. Each star in the cluster formed at roughly the same time. Comparing their different properties helps space scientists work out how stars evolve.

Stars are densest at the center of the Hercules Globular Cluster—more than **A HUNDRED TIMES** more crowded than the stars around **OUR SUN.**

STAR CITY
The Milky Way contains more than 150 known globular clusters. They orbit around the galaxy's central bulge. Looser groups of fewer stars, called open clusters, are found in the Milky Way's disk. Scientists estimate that there may be as many as 2,000 open clusters in the disk.

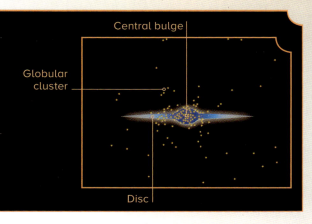
Central bulge / Globular cluster / Disc

LOCATION
The Hercules Globular Cluster is located in the constellation Hercules (the Strongman). It can sometimes be seen without a telescope in Northern Hemisphere skies, looking like a fuzzy star.

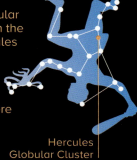
Hercules Globular Cluster

SIZE

The globular cluster is about **145 to 165 light years** across.

DISTANCE FROM EARTH
The cluster lies around **25,000 light years** from Earth.

AGE

Most of the stars in the Hercules Globular Cluster are thought to have formed about 13 billion years ago. The Universe itself is thought to be 13.8 billion years old. Our own sun is far younger, at around 4.6 billion years.

SUPER CLUSTER
Omega Centauri is the brightest and largest globular cluster in the Milky Way, containing around 10 million stars. The cluster, visible in Southern Hemisphere skies, appears almost as big as the moon.

COSMIC COLLISIONS
Stars in a globular cluster sometimes collide, producing neutron stars, black holes, or new stars known as blue stragglers.

Open Cluster
At the heart of the **Rosette Nebula,** around 5,000 light years from Earth, lies an open cluster of stars known as NGC 2244. An open cluster is a loose grouping of young stars, all born around the same time. Radiation from the stars in NGC 2244 causes the surrounding nebula to glow.

136 • ORION NEBULA

LOCATION
The Orion Nebula is one of the most observed objects in both the Southern and Northern Hemispheres. It can be seen by pointing a telescope toward the constellation Orion (the Hunter) with its center located just below Orion's Belt.

Orion Nebula

SIZE
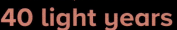
The nebula spans about **40 light years** across—a vast distance that far exceeds the size of our solar system.

DISTANCE FROM EARTH
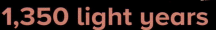
The Orion Nebula lies around **1,350 light years** from Earth, within our Milky Way galaxy.

DISCOVERED
This glowing area of sky was recorded by many ancient cultures, including the Maya. It was first cataloged by the French astronomer Nicolas-Claude Fabri de Peiresc in 1610.

AGE
Stars in the Trapezium Cluster are very young, with an average age of around **300,000 years.**

NEW PLANETS
It's not just stars that form in the nebula. Some stars gather disks of gas and dust, known as protoplanetary disks, that may eventually become planets.

TRAPEZIUM CLUSTER

The Orion Nebula houses the Trapezium Cluster, a group of massive young stars. Packed closely together, at least 1,000 stars fill an area of space similar to the gap between the sun and our next-nearest star system, Alpha Centauri.

The four **BRIGHT STARS** of the Trapezium Cluster form a four-sided shape—a trapezoid.

Cosmic Fire

THE ORION NEBULA IS EARTH'S CLOSEST MAJOR STAR NURSERY. It contains thousands of young stars, and thousands more that are yet to ignite. In this picture, hydrogen gas and dust glow orange, oxygen is green, and areas rich in sulfur appear red. The densest areas of gas and dust form mysterious dark pillars and arcs, carved by starlight and the stellar wind streaming from massive stars.

The Hubble Space Telescope took 520 photographs to create this billion-pixel image of a full moon-sized area of sky, with the **Orion Nebula** at the center.

Tiny **FAILED STARS** known as **brown dwarfs** have been seen in the **ORION NEBULA.**

ORION NEBULA • 137

Stellar winds from the massive stars collide with dust and gas from the nebula, creating these patterns.

Hundreds of **smaller stars** surround the central area. Some are so young, they are still hidden by dense disks of gas and debris, which will one day form solar systems.

A cluster of **massive stars** light up the surrounding gas and dust, making the center of the nebula glow brightly.

These faint red dots are **brown dwarfs.** They are hot, but not as hot as active stars.

138 • HORSEHEAD NEBULA

This hot blue supergiant is **Zeta Orionis**. It is the left-hand star of Orion's Belt.

The **Flame Nebula** is a star-forming region near the Horsehead Nebula.

Stars are forming inside the nebula, but most of them cannot be seen yet as they are surrounded by thick dust.

THE IMMENSE CLOUDS OF DUST AND GAS in this region of space are extremely faint, and the nearby bright stars make them even harder to see. To create this high-contrast image, the photographer combined data collected by very sensitive cameras over 30 hours.

Seahorse in the Sky

SILHOUETTED AGAINST A GLOWING INTERSTELLAR CLOUD, THE HORSEHEAD NEBULA IS ONE OF THE TOP TARGETS FOR TELESCOPES. Astronomers are watching how radiation from nearby stars is reshaping this dark, dense, cold clump of gas and dust. In around 5 million years, the seahorse-shaped pillar will disappear completely, gobbled up by newly forming stars inside it and then burned away by their light.

The **HORSEHEAD NEBULA** is a dark nebula visible to us because it **BLOCKS THE GLOW** from the nebula behind it.

There is no particular reason why the **NEBULA** looks like a seahorse— human brains like to spot patterns in chaos.

SWIRLING CLOUDS

To our eyes, which detect visible light, the dense, dark cloud looks like the silhouette of a seahorse. However, telescopes that detect other forms of light reveal more details. This infrared image taken by the Hubble Space Telescope shows how the gas and dust in the Horsehead Nebula fold and swirl.

HORSEHEAD NEBULA • 139

LOCATION
The Horsehead Nebula lies within the constellation Orion (the Hunter).

DISTANCE FROM EARTH
Between **1,300** and **1,400 light years** from Earth

SIZE
The Horsehead Nebula is **3½ light years** from top to bottom.

NAME
The Horsehead Nebula's official name is Barnard 33, as listed in an early catalog of dark clouds in space.

DISCOVERY
The clouds in this region of space were first spotted by German-British astronomer William Herschel in 1786. A little over 100 years later, Scottish astronomer Williamina Fleming noticed the intriguing horsehead detail on a photographic plate of the region.

GLOWING NEBULA
The intense red glow behind the Horsehead Nebula is caused by the emission nebula IC 434.

140 • RING NEBULA

LOCATION
The Ring Nebula is visible from Earth in the constellation Lyra (named after a lyre, a small musical instrument).

Ring Nebula

SIZE

The central blue ring is around 1 light year across.

DISTANCE FROM EARTH

The nebula lies around **2,300 light years** from Earth.

PLANETARY NEBULA
The Ring Nebula is a planetary nebula, one of the most colorful objects in the Universe. They are so called because to early astronomers they looked like faraway planets with glowing gas clouds.

COSMIC SHAPES
Planetary nebulas can be grouped into three main types:

SPHERICAL
Abell 39 is a near-spherical planetary nebula.

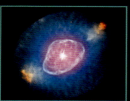
ELLIPTICAL
Like the Ring Nebula, the Blinking Planetary Nebula is elliptical (oval).

BIPOLAR
A bipolar nebula has two lobes of gas and dust.

BUILDING BLOCKS
Space dust detected in the Ring Nebula includes carbon-based molecules, which are key building blocks for life.

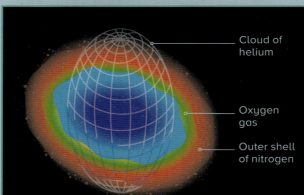

RING STRUCTURE
Although the Ring Nebula looks like a flat ring from Earth, it has a far more complex shape. A rugby ball-shaped cloud of superheated helium gas juts out either side of the squashed donut-shaped outer shell. Understanding this structure is helping space scientists to predict the future of our own medium-sized star, the Sun.

- Cloud of helium
- Oxygen gas
- Outer shell of nitrogen

Dying Star

MEDIUM-SIZED STARS FACE A SLOW BUT BEAUTIFUL ENDGAME. The stunning Ring Nebula formed as a dying star shed its outer layers—not in a supernova, but slowly over thousands of years. The glowing shell of gases includes elements forged inside the star and chemicals that have formed as this stardust is scattered across space. In this way, the end of one star provides the raw material for new solar systems.

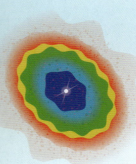

The gas shell **glows** because it has been heated to more than **17 TIMES** the temperature of the **SUN'S SURFACE.**

A **PLANETARY NEBULA** has a short **lifespan**—from a few thousand years to tens of thousands of years.

RING NEBULA • 141

The James Webb Space Telescope detected stripes around the edge of the **Ring Nebula**, like eyelashes around a cosmic eye. These are "shadows" cast by the clumps of denser gas, as they block the stream of light from the star.

Inside the ring's inner rim are **clumps of denser gas**. More than 20,000 have been counted, but scientists still aren't sure why they formed.

Only the core of the original star remains, but this **white dwarf** still burns at almost 180,000°F (100,000°C).

142 • BUTTERFLY NEBULA

LOCATION

The Butterfly Nebula is in the constellation Scorpius (the Scorpion).

SIZE
At its widest point, the nebula is more than **3 light years** across.

DISTANCE FROM EARTH
The nebula is around **3,800 to 4,000 light years** from Earth.

AGE

The nebula has been forming for more than **2,200 years.**

TEMPERATURE

The star at the heart of the nebula may have a surface temperature of more than **400,000°F (220,000°C).**

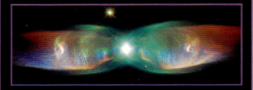

NAME
The Butterfly Nebula's official name is NGC 6302, which can help avoid confusion as there are other nebulas known as the Butterfly Nebula, including PN M2-9, above.

STAR MYSTERY
Much-anticipated images from the Webb telescope will reveal the central star. They may even show two stars merging.

Starlit Wings

THE SHIMMERING "WINGS" OF THE BUTTERFLY NEBULA REVEAL ITS HISTORY. Like other planetary nebulas, this giant cloud of gas and dust was ejected from a dying star. Although it is reaching the end of its life, this white dwarf is one of the hottest stars ever recorded. It bathes the nebula with intense radiation, making it glow brightly and showing us the paths taken by jets of gas speeding away from the star.

The nebula's dying star is about **TWO-THIRDS THE MASS OF OUR SUN** but over **200 times hotter.**

GAS JETS in the nebula move away from the star at almost **620,000 mph (1 million kph).**

WHITE DWARFS
The hidden star at the centre of the Butterfly Nebula is thought to be a white dwarf—a small, dense, incredibly hot star near the end of its life. The closest-known white dwarf to us is about 8.6 light years away and called Sirius B. It can be seen in this Hubble image as a tiny dot below and to the left of its companion star Sirius A, which is the brightest star in the night sky.

SIRIUS A AND SIRIUS B

BUTTERFLY NEBULA • 143

The reddish areas of this **Hubble Space Telescope image** reveal light emitted by nitrogen.

A belt of hot dust **hides the star** at the center of the nebula.

White regions reveal **shock waves** where fast-moving gas has collided with slower-moving gas ejected earlier from the star.

A PLANETARY NEBULA grows gradually, as a sunlike star swells up to become a red giant, then sheds its outer layers. The core contracts and heats up, releasing intense radiation that makes the nebula glow.

144 • STEPHAN'S QUINTET

LOCATION
Stephan's Quintet is located in the constellation Pegasus (the Flying Horse).

DISTANCE FROM EARTH
The compact group of four galaxies—NGC 7317, NGC 7318A, NGC 7318B, and NGC 7319—is almost 300 million light years from Earth. NGC 7320 is seven times closer, at around 40 million light years from Earth.

MASS
The supermassive black hole at the center of NGC 7319 has a mass 24 million times that of the sun.

ENERGY
Matter swirling into NGC 7319's black hole glows with the energy of 40 billion suns.

SHOCK WAVE
The shock wave created as NGC 7318B interacts with its three close galactic neighbors moves at 2 million mph (3.2 million kph).

DISCOVERY
French astronomer Edouard Stephan was the first to spot the group, in 1877. At that time, no one suspected there were galaxies beyond our own, so he recorded them as new nebulas.

X-RAY GALAXIES
By studying images of Stephan's Quintet taken in different wavelengths, such as x-rays and infrared, scientists can analyze how gravitational battles and energy blasts have shaped each galaxy over hundreds of millions of years. x-ray observations reveal the high-energy emissions from shock waves, while infrared images highlight regions of active star formation.

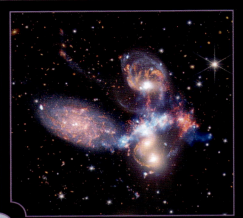

Interactions between the **galaxies** create **TIDAL TAILS,** where stars are ejected from the galaxies due to **GRAVITATIONAL FORCES.**

Dancing Galaxies

COLLIDING GALAXIES SPARKLE WITH NEWLY FORMING STARS. The five galaxies—three spiral and two elliptical—in this extraordinary image are known as Stephan's Quintet. Four of them are close enough to interact, which transforms their shape, stirs up dust, and sparks star formation. The area is a superb telescope target for scientists studying the evolution of galaxies and the creation of stars.

Scientists predict the **four close galaxies** will **MERGE INTO ONE LARGE ELLIPTICAL GALAXY** in several million years.

STEPHAN'S QUINTET • 145

At the center of spiral galaxy NGC 7319 is a supermassive **black hole** that eats up the surrounding matter.

These two small galaxies—the spiral NGC 7318B above the elliptical NGC 7318A—glow with the **reddish light of older stars**.

Spiral galaxy NGC 7320 is **hundreds of millions of light years closer** to Earth than the other galaxies in the group.

Galaxy NGC 7317 is **elliptical** (oval).

THIS IMAGE OF STEPHAN'S QUINTET was created from nearly a thousand separate images from the James Webb Space Telescope (JWST). It depicts an area spanning 620,000 light years and is one of the largest images ever taken by the JWST.

NGC 6670
A streak across space, this galaxy shines with over a hundred billion times the luminosity of the sun. This intense brightness is the result of two galaxies that collided in the past, triggering a frenzy of star formation. The centers of the two galaxies can still be identified, about 50,000 light years apart. On a galactic scale, this is more than close enough to pull them into a second collision.

ESO 593-8
Galaxies are mainly empty space. This allows the spiral galaxy that looks like a feather in this image to pierce another spiral galaxy in its path. Other images of ESO 593-8 have revealed a hidden third galaxy, where millions of new stars are forming.

UGC 8335
This squiggle in space shows how complex the effects of a galactic collision can be. Long, curved tails of stars and interstellar gas have been torn from the body of each spiral galaxy. Meanwhile, giant lanes of stardust streak across the galactic centers. In time, gravity will pull the stars from both galaxies into one giant elliptical cloud.

Colliding Galaxies

MANY DISTANT OBJECTS IN SPACE ARE MADE UP OF MULTIPLE GALAXIES, VIOLENTLY COLLIDING AND STEALING STARS FROM ONE ANOTHER. During these collisions, galaxies experience intense gravitational forces that alter their shapes, eject many stars, and pull others into new orbits. But galactic collisions and mergers don't just lead to destruction—they also trigger the birth of billions of new stars.

Astronomers think that the **Milky Way** and **Andromeda** galaxies may collide in around **4½ BILLION YEARS.**

COLLIDING GALAXIES • 147

ARP 272
The arms of two spiral galaxies, located within the Hercules Galaxy Cluster, are entangled as the galaxies collide and merge. This cosmic crash is happening about 450 million light years from Earth.

NGC 6240
This irregular galaxy is the result of a collision and merger between two galaxies. Hidden at its center are two supermassive black holes, which are only 3,000 light years apart and will one day collide.

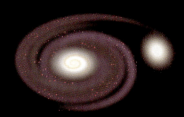

About a **QUARTER** of all galaxies are currently merging with other galaxies.

ARP 273
Hubble captured this image of two spiral galaxies after a close encounter. The shape of the arms suggests that the smaller galaxy once passed through the larger one, pulling both spirals out of shape.

ARP 148
Like an arrow hitting a bull's-eye, this spectacular collision is setting up shock waves that are pushing the contents of an entire galaxy outward into a ring shape. These two interacting galaxies are about 500 light years from Earth.

148 • WHIRLPOOL GALAXY

Each spiraling arm of the galaxy is a **star-forming factory**. The ends of the arms are very active areas.

A **supermassive black hole** at the heart of the galaxy is surrounded by older stars, which glow with a yellowish light.

The youngest, hottest star clusters are in the **blue-gray** patches.

THE WHIRLPOOL GALAXY is a spiral galaxy, like our Milky Way. Its curling arms are clearly defined. Scientists think that may be due to its interaction with the dwarf galaxy to its right.

SUPERNOVA

A powerful explosion of a dying star—known as a supernova—was noticed in the Whirlpool Galaxy in 2005. The supernova happened 24.7 million years ago, its burst of light taking that many years to reach Earth.

Supernova

WHIRLPOOL GALAXY • 149

Scientists believe that the **WHIRLPOOL GALAXY** is home to the first-known planet outside the Milky Way.

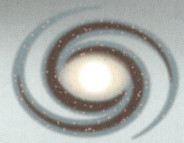

The Whirlpool Galaxy's glowing center is **100 MILLION TIMES BRIGHTER** than the sun.

Galactic Merger

BILLIONS OF NEW STARS BURST INTO LIFE WHEN GALAXIES COLLIDE. The Whirlpool Galaxy and its smaller companion began merging about 400 million years ago. Great clouds of gas and dust have been stirred up by this gravitational tug-of-war. As the clouds collapse under their own gravity, countless new stars ignite in clusters, lighting up the spiraling arms of the Whirlpool Galaxy.

LOCATION

The Whirlpool Galaxy lies in the constellation Canes Venatici (the Hunting Dogs).

SIZE
The Whirlpool Galaxy is about **60,000 light years** across.

DISTANCE FROM EARTH
Around **30 million light years**

AGE
Around **400 million years**

NAME

The Whirlpool Galaxy is also known as Messier 51a (M51a) or NGC 5194.

DISCOVERY
The Whirlpool Galaxy was discovered by French astronomer Charles Messier in 1773.

COSMIC COMPANION
The Whirlpool Galaxy's companion dwarf galaxy is called Messier 51b (M51b) or NGC 5195. It was discovered by French astronomer Pierre Méchain in 1781. This smaller galaxy's gravitational force creates waves in the Whirlpool, triggering the formation of stars.

150 • NEUTRON STARS

AVERAGE SIZE
Neutron stars are about **13.7 miles** (22 km) in diameter—the size of a big city.

MASS

A typical neutron star packs the mass of up to two suns.

FAST SPINNERS
As its core shrinks, a neutron star may spin faster and faster. Some neutron stars rotate as fast as 700 times a second.

LIGHTHOUSES
Some neutron stars are like space lighthouses. As they spin, they emit beams of electromagnetic waves (x-rays or radio waves), which can be detected on Earth. These flashing neutron stars are known as pulsars.

SUPER-STRONG STARS
The solid surface of a neutron star is estimated to be as much as 10 billion times stronger than steel.

GOLD MINE

Scientists estimate that the neutron star collision that was observed in 2017 created 200 Earth masses of pure gold.

EXPANDING CLOUD
When two neutron stars crash into each other, they throw out a cloud of radioactive debris, which expands from the size of a city to the size of our solar system in just one day.

INSIDE A NEUTRON STAR
A neutron star's solid crust is about 0.6 miles (1 km) thick. This layer is incredibly smooth—any bumps are less than 0.19 in (5 mm) tall. Beneath the crust lies a superfluid interior made up of subatomic particles called neutrons.

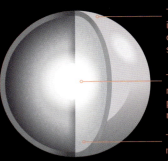

- The outer layer is solid, including a thin crust of super-dense iron.
- The core is made up of protons and neutrons.
- The inner layer mainly consists of neutrons.

NEUTRON STARS are the most powerful **magnets** in the universe—their magnetic field may be a **TRILLION TIMES** stronger than Earth's.

Space Shakers

WITNESS THE MOST POWERFUL AND VIOLENT COLLISION IN THE UNIVERSE.
Neutron stars form when a giant star dies in a supernova explosion, leaving behind a small, hot, and incredibly dense core with a very powerful gravitational field. When two neutron stars collide, they release enough energy to ripple the fabric of space itself. These spectacular collisions also create heavy metals, including gold, silver, platinum, and uranium.

A tablespoon of **NEUTRON STAR weighs** about the same as **QOMOLANGMA FENG** (Mount Everest).

NEUTRON STARS 151

The explosion releases a short burst of the highest-energy light, known as a **gamma-ray burst.**

After two neutron stars begin orbiting one another, their intense gravitational effects draw them together in a **violent collision.**

THE NEUTRON STARS depicted in this illustration probably spent 11 billion years orbiting each other before finally colliding. The explosive event was detected in 2017, about 130 million light years from Earth.

152 ● BLACK HOLES

Invisible Force

NOTHING CAN ESCAPE FROM THE INSIDE OF A BLACK HOLE. With no light able to leave their surfaces to reach our telescopes, black holes are completely invisible. Most of what we know about them is based on theory rather than observation, and many mysteries remain. However, scientists can detect the effects of a black hole's enormous gravity on nearby stars.

A BLACK HOLE is one of the most fascinating objects in the universe. The illustration here shows a black hole surrounded by glowing gas and dust spiralling inward toward the event horizon.

Even the fastest thing in the Universe—light—**CANNOT ESCAPE** from the inside of a black hole.

The **event horizon** marks the "surface" of the black hole. Once matter or light is inside the event horizon, it can never escape.

SIZE
Despite packing in unimaginable mass, the singularity at the center of a black hole would fit in the palm of your hand.

MASS
M87 is a galaxy with is one of the largest black holes ever detected at its center. Called M87*, it is more than 1000 times the mass of Sagittarius A*, the black hole at the center of the Milky Way. M87* is located 55 million light years from Earth.

DIAMETER
Sagittarius A* has a diameter of about 15 million miles (24 million km). At 24 billion miles (38 billion km), M87*'s diameter is more than 1,500 times bigger. Shown here is a size comparison of the two black holes and our sun.

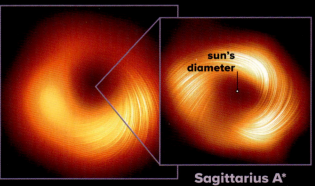

M87*

sun's diameter

Sagittarius A*

BLACK HOLES · 153

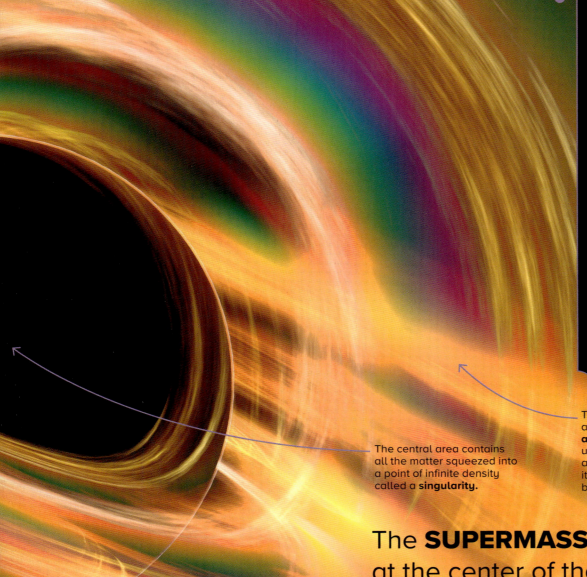

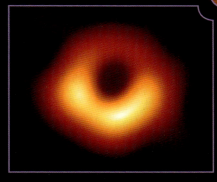

THE FIRST IMAGE

In 2019, the first-ever image showing the presence of a black hole was taken by the planet-sized Event Horizon Telescope (an array of eight radio telescopes dotted around Earth's surface). The image shows the shape of the supermassive black hole M87* at the center of the M87 galaxy. The black hole is silhouetted by glowing matter that is yet to pass the event horizon.

This cloud of gas and dust is called the **accretion disk**. It heats up due to gravitational and frictional forces as it moves closer to the black hole.

The central area contains all the matter squeezed into a point of infinite density called a **singularity**.

The **SUPERMASSIVE** black hole at the center of the galaxy **Holm 15a** is about **40 BILLION** times the mass of the sun.

TYPES OF BLACK HOLE

- **STELLAR MASS BLACK HOLE**
  When the most massive type of star dies in a supernova, its outer layers are scattered across space. The inner layers collapse into a compact core of infinite density known as a singularity.

- **SUPERMASSIVE BLACK HOLE**
  This forms in the spaces between stars, when vast clouds of gas collapse under their own gravity. This type of black hole is found at the center of most galaxies and also has a singularity.

COSMIC COLLISION

Albert Einstein's general theory of relativity predicted how black holes are structured. Einstein also correctly predicted that when two black holes merge, the violent collision sends gravitational waves rippling through the fabric of space.

TIME STOPS

The closer you get to a black hole, the slower the time gets. What happens inside the black hole is still a mystery.

Glossary

ACCRETION DISK A swirling ring of gas and dust that forms around a star or black hole. As material in the disk gets pulled toward the center, it heats up and glows.

ANTENNA A type of aerial used on spacecraft and telescopes to send and receive signals.

ASTEROID A rocky object smaller than a planet. Most asteroids orbit the sun between Mars and Jupiter.

ASTEROID BELT The area of space in the solar system, between the orbits of Mars and Jupiter, that has the highest number of orbiting asteroids in it.

ATMOSPHERE The layer of gas that surrounds a planet or star.

AURORA A pattern of light that appears near the poles of some planets.

BIG BANG The cosmic expansion that scientists believe created the universe billions of years ago.

BIODIVERSITY The variety of life on Earth. An area with high biodiversity has lots of different kinds of animals and plants.

BLACK HOLE An area of space with such a strong gravitational pull that it sucks in anything that comes too close, even light.

BROWN DWARF An object that is smaller than a star but larger than a planet. It produces heat, but little to no light at all. Also known as a failed star.

CALDERA A large crater left after a violent eruption destroys a volcano.

CANYON A deep, steep-sided valley, often with cliffs on both sides.

CAPSULE A small spacecraft designed to carry astronauts back to Earth from space.

CELESTIAL OBJECT Any natural object seen outside Earth's atmosphere.

CLIMATE The typical annual pattern of weather in a specific location.

COMA A glowing cloud of gas and dust around a comet.

COMET A large solid object made of dust and ice that orbits the sun. As it gets near the sun, the ice starts to evaporate, creating two tails: one of dust and another of gas.

CONSTELLATION A named area of the sky with a distinctive pattern of stars.

CORE The central part of a planet or star.

CORONA The outermost part of the sun or a star's atmosphere, seen as a white halo during a solar eclipse.

COSMOS Another word for the universe.

CRATER A bowl-shaped depression on the surface of a planet, moon, asteroid, or other body.

CRUST The hard, usually rocky, outermost layer of Earth or another planet or moon.

CRYOVOLCANO Also called an ice volcano, a type of volcano that erupts liquids and gases when frozen water or other forms of ice melt.

CRYSTAL A small piece of a solid material that naturally forms a regular shape with flat sides and straight edges.

DARK MATTER Invisible material believed to exist in space. Astrophysicists think that dark matter and dark energy make up 95 percent of the universe.

DARK NEBULA A cloud of gas or dust in space that blocks the light from stars behind it.

DAY The time it takes for a planet to rotate once on its axis.

DEEP FIELD An image of a part of the sky that reveals very faint and distant objects.

DRONE A small robotic flying vehicle.

DWARF GALAXY A small galaxy with about 1,000 to a few billion stars.

DWARF PLANET A small, spherical planet that does not have enough mass and gravity to clear its path around the sun of debris.

EARTHSHINE Light that is scattered off the clouds, oceans, and land of our planet into space, where it can faintly illuminate the night-side of the moon.

ECLIPSE A brief event when one astronomical body, such as the moon, casts a shadow on another astronomical object, such as Earth.

ELECTROMAGNETIC WAVE A type of energy wave that can travel through space. Radio waves, visible light, and x-rays are forms of electromagnetic wave.

ELLIPTICAL GALAXY A type of galaxy that has a rounded shape similar to a sphere, or sometimes a football. Elliptical galaxies don't have spiral arms like the Milky Way.

EMISSION NEBULA A cloud of gas in space that emits light.

ESA European Space Agency; an international space exploration organization with 22 European member countries.

EVENT HORIZON The boundary around a black hole; nothing can escape from the black hole after crossing it.

EXOPLANET A planet that orbits a star other than the sun.

EXTINCTION The permanent loss of a species (type of organism) after its last living member dies.

FAILED STAR A term sometimes given to a brown dwarf.

FERMI BUBBLES Two vast bubbles of hot gas that extend above and below the center of our galaxy.

FLYBY When a spacecraft flies past a planet, comet, or asteroid without landing or orbiting it.

GALAXY A collection of stars—from about 1,000 to trillions—gas, and dust held together by gravity.

GALILEAN MOON One of the four largest moons of the planet Jupiter (Io, Europa, Ganymede, and Callisto). They are known as Galilean moons because they were first seen by the Italian astronomer Galileo Galilei.

GAMMA RAY The most powerful form of electromagnetic radiation, with the shortest wavelength. Gamma rays are produced by the most energetic objects in the universe.

GLOBULAR CLUSTER A large, ball-shaped cluster of old stars tightly packed together.

GRAVITATIONAL WAVE A wave that travels through a gravitational field at the speed of light. Gravitational waves are caused by violent cosmic events, such as collisions between black holes.

GRAVITY The force that pulls all objects that have mass and energy toward one another. It is the force that keeps moons in orbit around planets, and planets in orbit around the sun.

GLOSSARY 155

HABITABLE ZONE The area of a solar system in which liquid water can exist on a planet, making life possible.

HEAT SHIELD A part of a spacecraft that protects other parts from the heat of the sun or the heat of an engine.

HERBIG-HARO (HH) OBJECT A bright patch of gas and dust near a newborn star.

HURRICANE A large, rotating storm with powerful winds and bands of clouds spiraling out from its center.

HYPERNOVA An unusually powerful supernova (exploding star).

HYPERSONIC More than five times faster than the speed of sound.

IMPACT CRATER Large hole left in a planet or moon's surface by a fast-moving object, such as an asteroid, crashing into it.

INTERSTELLAR Between the stars.

IRREGULAR GALAXY A galaxy with no clear shape.

JAXA Japan Aerospace Exploration Agency; Japan's national space agency.

KUIPER BELT A large expanse of the solar system beyond the orbit of the planet Neptune that contains many small, frozen bodies, known as Kuiper Belt Objects.

LANDER A spacecraft designed to land on the surface of a planet or other space object.

LAUNCH When a spacecraft leaves Earth and reaches the speed in space at which it can remain in orbit.

LAVA Molten rock that erupts from a volcano.

LIGHT YEAR The distance that light travels in one year (about 6 trillion miles or 10 trillion km).

LUMINOSITY The brightness of something, such as a star.

LUNAR Relating to the moon.

LUNAR ECLIPSE An event during which Earth casts a shadow on the moon.

LUNAR SOIL The thick layer of dust and rock fragments that covers the moon's surface.

MAGNETIC FIELD An area of magnetism created by a planet, star, or galaxy, which surrounds it and extends into space.

MAGNETIC POLE The northern or southern end of a planet's magnetic field or one end of a magnet.

MAGNETOMETER An instrument that is used to measure magnetic forces.

MANTLE A thick layer of hot rock underneath the crust of a moon or planet.

MARE (PLURAL MARIA) A large, dark area on the moon's surface that has few craters. Also called a lunar sea, a mare is formed from floods of lava.

METEOR The scientific name for a shooting star. A tiny fleck of space dust that shines briefly as it burns when colliding with Earth's atmosphere.

METEORITE A space rock, or a fragment of a space rock, that has made it through Earth's atmosphere to land on the surface.

METEOROID A small piece of rock, metal, or ice travelling through space.

MICROGRAVITY Very weak gravity on a spaceship, making objects float as though weightless.

MICROSHUTTER ARRAY A grid of 248,000 tiny shutters on the James Webb Space Telescope that can be opened to collect data on hundreds of different objects in view at the same time.

MILKY WAY The name of the galaxy that contains our solar system.

MINERAL A natural, inorganic solid substance. Rocks are made of minerals.

MODULE A distinct part of a spacecraft or space station.

NASA National Aeronautics and Space Administration; the agency of the United States government with responsibility for the nation's space programme.

NEAR-EARTH ASTEROID An asteroid on an orbital path that comes close to Earth.

NEBULA A huge cloud of gas and dust in space.

NEUTRON One of the tiny particles found in the nucleus (center) of an atom.

NEUTRON STAR A dense collapsed star that is mainly made of neutrons.

NUCLEAR FUSION A process in which two atomic nuclei join to form a heavier nucleus and release large amounts of energy.

NUCLEUS (OF A COMET) The solid core of a comet.

OBSERVATORY A building, spacecraft, or satellite containing a telescope that is used for observing objects in space.

OORT CLOUD A huge sphere of icy, cometlike objects that is believed to surround the sun and form the outermost region of the solar system.

OPEN CLUSTER A loosely packed group of usually young stars within a galaxy.

ORBIT The curved path taken by an object in space as it travels around a larger object. Earth orbits the sun, for example.

ORBITAL PERIOD The time taken for an object in space to make one complete orbit of another object. The orbital period of a planet around the sun is called a year.

ORBITER A spacecraft that is designed to orbit an object but not land on it.

ORGANIC SUBSTANCE A substance derived from living organisms or a compound containing carbon atoms.

PALLASITE A type of meteorite that has large crystals embedded in metal.

PHASE The portion of a moon or planet that is seen to be lit by the sun. The moon passes through a cycle of different phases every 30 days.

PLANET A spherical object that orbits a star and is sufficiently massive (unlike a dwarf planet) to have cleared its orbital path of debris.

PLANETARY NEBULA A glowing cloud of gas around a star at the end of its life.

PLANETESIMALS Small rocky or icy objects that are pulled together by gravity to form planets.

GLOSSARY

PLASMA A state of matter in which a gas becomes so hot that its atoms split into charged particles (ions).

PROBE An uncrewed spacecraft that is designed to explore objects in space and transmit information back to Earth.

PROMINENCE A huge, flamelike loop of plasma that erupts from the surface of the sun.

PROTON A positively charged particle found in the nucleus (center) of atoms.

PROTOPLANETARY DISK A huge, roughly flat, expanse of gas and dust orbiting a young star. Planets can form from these disks.

PROTOSTAR A star in the early stages of formation, consisting of the center of a collapsed cloud that is heating up and growing by adding surrounding matter.

PULSAR A neutron star that sends out pulses of radiation as it spins.

RADAR The use of radio waves and their reflections to detect and study distant objects.

RADIATION Energy released by an object either in the form of electromagnetic waves (such as light) or as particles.

RADIO WAVE A type of electromagnetic wave that has low energy and a long wavelength. A radio telescope is used to detect radio waves from distant stars and galaxies.

RADIOACTIVE A radioactive substance consists of unstable atoms that break up, releasing powerful radiation as they do so.

RE-ENTRY When a spacecraft re-enters Earth's atmosphere from space.

RED GIANT A large star with a relatively low surface temperature, giving it a slightly reddish color. A red giant is nearing the final stage of its life.

RED NOVA An explosion that occurs when two stars merge. Red novas produce a distinct reddish light.

ROSCOSMOS Russia's national space agency.

ROVER A robotic, wheeled vehicle used to explore the surface of a planet or moon.

SATELLITE A spacecraft placed into orbit around Earth, or any natural object that orbits a planet, star, or galaxy.

SHOCK WAVE A wave of energy that is produced by an explosion or by something travelling at supersonic speed.

SINGULARITY A point in space where matter is compressed by gravity into an infinitely small space. Singularities are found in black holes.

SOLAR ARRAY A set of solar panels used to generate electricity from sunlight.

SOLAR FLARE The brightening of a part of the sun's surface, accompanied by a release of huge amounts of electromagnetic energy.

SOLAR PANEL A device used to generate electricity from sunlight.

SOLAR PARTICLE A high-energy, charged particle emitted by the sun.

SOLAR SYSTEM The sun and the planets, moons, and other objects that orbit it.

SPACECRAFT A vehicle, either crewed or robotic, that is designed to travel through space.

SPACETIME A combination of the three dimensions of space (length, breadth, and height) with the dimension of time.

SPACEWALK Any activity in which an astronaut in a spacesuit goes outside a spacecraft during a mission. Also called an EVA (extravehicular activity).

SPIRAL GALAXY A kind of galaxy that has a flat, circular disk composed of whirlpool-like structures, known as spiral arms. The Milky Way and the nearby Andromeda Galaxy are both examples of spiral galaxies.

STAR A gigantic ball of gas that generates light and heat.

STAR NURSERY An area where new stars are forming. Also called stellar nurseries, star nurseries are typically found in large clouds of gas and dust (nebulas).

STELLAR Relating to stars.

STELLAR WIND A flow of charged particles from a star. The sun's stellar wind is known as the solar wind.

SUBATOMIC PARTICLE Any particle smaller than an atom.

SUN-SHIELD A heat shield that protects instruments on a spacecraft from the sun's heat and light.

SUPERFLUID A special kind of fluid that can flow with no resistance.

SUPERGIANT An extremely large and bright star.

SUPERMASSIVE BLACK HOLE A black hole with a mass hundreds of thousands, millions, or billions of times greater than our sun.

SUPERNOVA A very bright explosion that happens when a massive star dies.

TECTONIC PLATE One of the gigantic fragments that makes up Earth's outermost rocky layer. Tectonic plates move slowly, changing the shapes of continents and causing earthquakes and volcanoes.

TELESCOPE An instrument used to magnify and view distant objects.

ULTRAVIOLET RADIATION An invisible form of light emitted by the sun that has a wavelength shorter than visible light but longer than x-rays.

UNIVERSE Everything in space, including all of the stars, nebulas, and galaxies.

VISIBLE LIGHT Electromagnetic radiation that our eyes can detect, giving us the sense of vision.

WAVELENGTH The length of waves in any kind of energy transmitted as waves.

WHITE DWARF A small, dim star. Our sun will eventually become a white dwarf.

X-RAY Electromagnetic radiation with wavelengths shorter than ultraviolet radiation but longer than gamma rays.

YEAR The time taken for a planet to make one complete orbit of the sun.

Index

Page numbers in **bold** refer to main entries.

A

Abell 39 Nebula 140
accretion disks 153
Ahuna Mons, cryovolcano 57
Akatsuki orbiter, image taken by 20
Aldrin, Edwin "Buzz" 40, 41, 42
Alpha Centauri 136
ammonia 80, 83
Andromeda Galaxy 119, 146
animals 24, 26, 58
Antarctica 26
Apophis, asteroid 65
Ariane 5 rocket 102
Armstrong, Neil 40, 41
ARP 148 Galaxy 147
ARP 272 Galaxy 147
ARP 273 Galaxy 147
Arrokoth 91
Artemis Program 40, **44–5**
Asteroid Belt 56, 57, 59
    and meteorites 60
asteroids **58–9**, 67, 88
    Asteroid Belt 56, 57, 59, 60
    impacts by 58, 60, 67
    missions to 64, 65
astronauts
    exercising 34
    experiments, conducting 33, 34
    International Space Station (ISS) 31, 32, 33, **34–5**
    moon missions 41–5, 62
    repairing Hubble Space Telescope 118, 119, 121
    training 62
astronomers 15, 56
    and galaxies 119, 144, 149
    Herbig-Haro (HH) objects 129
    and nebulas 110, 122, 127, 136, 139
    Pluto, discovery of 85
atmosphere
    and auroras 30, 31
    Earth 24, 25, 30
    exoplanets 130
    Jupiter 66
    Mars 46
    moons 77
    Pluto 85
    sun 6, 10
    Venus 20
auroras
    brown dwarfs 100–1
    Earth **30–1**
    Jupiter 31, 66
    Neptune 31
    Uranus 80, 81

B

Barringer Crater 62–3
BD+60°2522 127
Bennu, asteroid 64
BepiColombo 18–19
Bernardinelli-Bernstein, Comet 87
Big Bang 99
bipolar nebulas 140
Birkeland, Kristian 31
black holes 133, **152–3**
    M87* 152, 153
    Sagittarius A* 152
    supermassive 92, 144, 147, 148, 153
Blinking Planetary Nebula 140
blue stragglers 133
Bok, Bart 129
brown dwarfs **100–1**, 107, 136, 137
Bubble Nebula **126–7**
Butterfly Nebula **142–3**

C

Callisto 70
Caloris Basin Crater **16–17**
canyons 46, 50, 76, 84
carbon
    comets 87
    heat shields, probe 11
    Mercury 14
    Ring Nebula 140
carbon dioxide
    Earth 25
    Mars 46, 51
    Venus 20
carbon monoxide 125
Carina Nebula 108
Cartwheel Galaxy 106
Cassini **78–9**
    images by 72, **74–5**, 77
Cassini Division 73
Cassini-Huygens mission **78–9**
Cassiopeia A, supernova remnant 107
Ceres **56–7**
Charon 85, 91
cities 26
cliffs 76, 80
clouds
    black holes 153
    Earth 24, 28
    exoplanets 130, 131
    galaxies 93, 94, 146, 149
    Herbig-Haro (HH) objects 124, 129
    Jupiter 67
    nebulas 108, 110, **112–13**, 115, 122, 124, 127, 139, 140, 142
    Neptune 82, 83
    neutron stars 150
    Saturn 78

supernova-blast clouds 107
    Uranus 80, 81
    Venus 20, 21
clusters, star 107, **132–5**, 136, 137
Colombo, Giuseppe (Bepi) 19
comets 10, **86–7**
    hitting planets 14, 44, 67
    nucleus 86, 87
    rings, planetary 73
    Rosetta mission **88–9**
Crab Nebula **122–3**
craters
    asteroids 59
    Ceres 57
    Earth 62
    Mars 50, 55
    Mercury 14, 15, 17
    moons 36, 70, 76, 77
    Venus 20
cryovolcanoes 57, 76, 84, 85
Culann Patera 70

D

Dactyl 59
Daphnis 77
dark matter 92
Dawn 56, 57
Deep Field **98–9**, 119
Deimos 47
deserts 26
Dione 76
drones 55
dust devils **48–9**
dwarf planets 56, 84–5, 90–1

E

Eagle Nebula **114–17**
Earth **24–31**
    and asteroids 58, 59, 60, 61, 64
    life on 6, **26–7**, 58
    storms **28–9**
    tides 36
earthquakes 25
eclipses 9, **38–9**
Einstein, Albert 153
elements
    Earth's core 61
    lightest in the universe 6
    meteorites 61
    Pluto's core 84
    stars 140
elliptical galaxies 98, 144, 145
elliptical nebulas 140
Enceladus 76
energy
    auroras 31
    black holes 144
    creation of the universe 99
    Fermi Bubbles 92
    hurricanes on Earth 28

stars 6, 31, 108, 144, 150, 151
    sun 6, 31
Eros, asteroid 58
ESO 593-8 Galaxy 146
ethyl formate 92
Europa 71
Event Horizon Telescope 153
event horizons 152
exoplanets 118, **130–1**
    and water 118
experiments
    Artemis 44
    International Space Station (ISS) 33, 34
    Perseverance, Mars rover 54
    Philae, comet lander 89
exploration *see* missions, data-collecting

FG

Fabri de Peiresc, Nicolas-Claude 136
Fermi Bubbles 92
Flame Nebula 138
Fleming, Williamina 139
flybys
    BepiColombo 19
    Cassini-Huygens 78
    Rosetta 88
Fukang meteorite 60
galaxies
    ancient 98–9
    Andromeda 119, 146
    Cartwheel 106
    clusters 99
    colliding 92, 106, 128, **144–7**
    elliptical 98, 144, 145, 146
    Milky Way **92–5**, 146
    most distant 103
    spiral **92–3**, 118, 144, 145, 146, 147, **148–9**
    Whirlpool **148–9**
Galileo Galilei 70
Galileo spacecraft 59
gamma-ray bursts 151
Ganymede 71
Gaspra, asteroid 59
gemstones 61
gold 103, 150
gravity
    comets 86, 87
    galaxies 99, 146, 149
    moon, Earth's 36
    rings around planets 73, 74
    stars 6, 114, 115, 129, 144, 150, 151
    sun 6
Great Dark Spot 82, 83
Great Red Spot **68–9**
Green, Comet 87

158 ● INDEX

H

habitable zone 24, 131
Haro, Guillermo 129
Hayabusa spacecraft 58, 59, 65
HD189733b, exoplanet 131
HD209458b, exoplanet 130
heat shields 10, 11, 19, 79, 103
helium
    nebulas 127, 140
    planets 66, 80
    sun 6
Herbig, George 129
Herbig-Haro (HH) objects **124–5**, **128–9**
Hercules Globular Cluster **132–3**, 147
Herschel Crater 77
Herschel, William 127, 139
HH 46/47 **128–9**
HH 211 **124–5**
Homunculus Nebula 108
Horsehead Nebula **138–9**
Hubble, Edwin 119
Hubble Space Telescope **118–21**
    Deep Field 99, 119
    images by 109, 111, 118, 119, 126, 132, 136, 139, 142, 143, 147
    repairs by astronauts 118, 119, 121
hurricanes **28–9**
Huygens 78, 79
hydrogen
    aurora, Earth's 30
    Jupiter 66
    nebulas 113, 115, 123, 126, 127, 136
    stars 6, 125
    Uranus 80
Hyperion 76
hypernovas 108

I

Iapetus 76, 77
IC 348 star cluster 107
IC 434 emission nebula 139
Ida, asteroid 59
infrared light 106, 124
    auroras 80
    brown dwarfs 100
    telescopes 100, 103, 114, 115, 118, 123
Ingenuity drone 55
International Space Station (ISS) **32–3**, 34–5
    and auroras 31
    modules 32, 33
    orbital period 32
    speed of 33
Io 70, 91
iron
    Earth 24
    Mars 46, 47, 51
    meteorites 60, 61
    moon, Earth's 37
    stars 150
Itokawa, asteroid 58, 65

JKL

JADES-GS-z14-0 Galaxy 103
James Webb Space Telescope (JWST) 100, **102–5**
    Deep Field **98–9**
    images from 81, 83, 98, 106–7, 112, 115, 123, 124, 128, 129, 141, 145
jet streams 67
jets of gas from protostars 124, 125, 129
Jupiter **66–71**
    auroras 31
    moons **70–1**
    rings 73
Kepler 186f 131
Kibō laboratory, ISS 33
Kuiper Belt 86, 91
laboratories, ISS 33
landers 78, 79, 88, 89
Leonard, Comet 86
life 24, 26–7
    molecules for 59, 65, 140
light, and black holes 152

M

M87*, black hole 152, 153
Maat Mons volcano **22–3**
Magellan mission 20, 22
magnetic field
    Earth 24, 31
    neutron stars 150
    Pillars of Creation 114, 115
    sun 10
mapping
    67P/Churyumov-Gerasimenko Comet 88
    Mercury 14, 18
Mars **46–55**
    exploration of **54–5**
    moons 47
Mars Express orbiter, images taken by 47, 52
Mars Recconaissance Orbiter 48
mass
    black holes 92, 144, 152, 153
    galaxies 99
    neutron stars 150
    pulsars 122
    sun 7
Méchain, Pierre 149
Mercury **14–19**
Messenger 14, 19
Messier 51b Galaxy 149
Messier, Charles 149
meteorites 14, 20, 36, **60–1**
meteoroids 61, 62
meteors 60, 61, 62
methane 77, 80, 81, 83, 85
microgravity 34
Milky Way **92–5**
    collision with Andromeda Galaxy 146
    exoplanets 130
    nebulas **112–15**
    star clusters 133

Mimas 77
minerals
    asteroids 58, 65
    dwarf planets 56, 57
    planets 47, 60
    needed for life 65
    meteorites 60
Miranda 80
mirrors, telescope 98, 102, 103, 105, 118, 119
missions, data-collecting
    to asteroids 59, **64–5**
    to Ceres 56
    to a comet 88
    to Mars 54, 55
    to Mercury **18–19**
    to the moon **40–1, 44–5**
    to Neptune 82
    to Pluto **90–1**
    to Saturn **78–9**
    to the sun **10–11**
    to Titan 79
    to Venus 22
moon, Earth's **36–9**
    astronauts on the 40–5
    and eclipses 9, 38–9
    effect on Earth 24, 36
moons
    and asteroids 59
    eclipses 9
    of Jupiter **70–1**
    of Mars 47
    of Neptune 82, 83
    of Pluto 85, 91
    of Saturn **76–7**
    of Uranus 80, 81
    see also moon, Earth's
mountains 20
Musgrave, Story 121

N

NEAR Shoemaker 58
nebulas 7, 113, 115, 128
    Abell 39 140
    Blinking Planetary 140
    Bubble **126–7**
    Butterfly **142–3**
    Crab **122–3**
    Eagle **114–17**
    Flame 138
    Homunculus 108
    Horsehead **138–9**
    IC 434 139
    NGC 604 107
    Orion **136–7**
    planetary 140, 143
    Ring **140–1**
    Rosette 134
    Serpens 106
    Swiss cheese 111
    Tarantula 106
Neptune **82–3**
    auroras 31
    moons 82, 83
    rings 73, 83
neutron stars 122, 133, **150–1**
neutrons 150

New Horizons 84, **90–1**
NGC 604 Nebula 107
NGC 1512 Galaxy 118
NGC 2244 open cluster **134–5**
NGC 6240 Galaxy 147
NGC 6670 Galaxy 146
NGC 7317 Galaxy 144, 145
NGC 7318a Galaxy 144, 145
NGC 7318b Galaxy 144, 145
NGC 7319 Galaxy 144, 145
NGC 7320 Galaxy 144, 145
nitrogen
    Earth 25, 30
    nebulas 126, 127, 140, 143
    Pluto 85, 90
nuclear fuel 55

O

Occator Crater 57
oceans 27, 36, 71, 76
Olympus Mons 46, 50
Omega Centauri 133
Oort Cloud 86
Opportunity rover, image by 50
orbiters
    Akatsuki, image taken by 20
    BepiColombo 18, 19
    Mars Express, images taken by 47, 52
    Mars Recconaissance, image taken by 48
    Rosetta 88, 89
Orion Nebula **136–7**
Orion spacecraft 44, 45
Orion Spur 92
OSIRIS-APEX 65
OSIRIS-REx **64–5**
oxygen
    Earth 24, 25, 30
    nebulas 126, 136, 140
    spacecraft 40, 46

P

Pallas, Peter 61
pallasites 60, 61
Pan 77
Parker, Eugene 10
Parker Solar Probe **10–11**
Parsons, William 122
peridot 61
Perseverance rover **54–5**
Philae 88, 89
Phobos 47
Phoebe 76
Piazzi, Giuseppe 56
Pillars of Creation **114–15**, 116
planetary nebulas 140, 142, 143
planetesmals 60
planets
    creation of 136
    Earth **24–31**
    exoplanets 118, **130–1**
    fastest in the solar system 14
    having most moons 76
    Jupiter 31, **66–71**, 73

INDEX • 159

Mars **46–55**
Mercury **14–19**
Neptune 31, 73, **82–3**
Saturn **72–9**
Uranus **80–1**
Venus 10, **20–3**
water on 14, 25, 118
in Whirlpool Galaxy 149
plants
on Earth 26, 27
vegetables, growing in space 33
Pluto **84–5**
New Horizons mission **90–1**
plutonium, and spacecraft 90
probes
Parker Solar Probe **10–11**
Rosetta **88–9**
Voyager 2 82
prominences 6
protons 150
protoplanetary disks 136
protostars 107, 112–13, 116
Herbig-Haro 211 **124–5**
Herbig-Haro 46/47 **128–9**
pulsars 122, 123, 150

R

radio waves 79, 124, 150
radioactive
debris 150
elements 84
plutonium 90
rocks 56
rainforest, Amazon 27
red giants 7, 143
red nova explosions 111
Rheasilvia Crater 59
Rho Ophiuchi **112–13**
Ring Nebula **140–1**
ringed planets 72, 73, **74–5**, 76, 81, 83
rivers 26, 77
robotic arms 33, 54, 65, 121
robots, on Mars 46, **54–5**
rockets
Ariane 5 102
Saturn V 40
Space Launch System (SLS) 44
rocks
asteroids 56, **58–9**, 64
Earth 24
Mars 55
Mercury 14
meteorites **60–1**
moon, Earth's 36
Rosetta **88–9**
Rosette Nebula 134
rovers
Opportunity, image by 50
Perseverance 46, **54–5**
Ryugu, asteroid 59

S

S1 star 112
Sagittarius A* 92, 93, 152
sand dunes 50, 51

Santa Maria Crater 50
Saturn **72–9**
exploration of **78–9**
moons **76–7**
rings 72, 73, **74–5**
storms 73
Serpens Nebula 106
shock waves
from colliding galaxies 144, 147
from gas ejected by stars 124, 125, 143
singularities 152, 153
Sirius A 142
Sirius B 142
Skycrane 54
SMACS 0723 galaxy cluster 98, 99
solar eclipses 9
solar panels
spacecraft 32, 55, 89
telescopes 103, 118, 119
solar particles 30, 31
solar system **4–93**
asteroids 56, **58–9**
comets **86–7**, 88–9
cryovolcanoes 57, 76, 84, 85
dwarf planets 56–7, 84–5
exploration 10–11, 18–19, 40–1, 44–5, 54–5, 64–5, 78–9, 88–9, 90–1
and the Milky Way 92
moons 36–45, 47, 59, 70–1, 76–7, 79, 80, 81, 82, 83, 85
planets 7, 14–15, 20–31, 37, 46–55, 66–9, 72–5, 80–3
storm, largest 68
sun **6–7**
volcanoes 20, 21, 22, 46, 50, 70, 91
solar systems, forming 137, 140
spacecraft
Apollo **40–1**
Artemis **44–5**
BepiColombo **18–19**
Cassini-Huygens **78–9**
drones 55
landers 78, 79, 88, 89
most distant object explored by 91
orbiters 18, 19, 48, 88, 89
Orion 44, 45
OSIRIS-APEX 65
OSIRIS-REx **64–5**
probes **10–11**, 82, **88–9**
rockets 40, 44, 102
rovers 46, 50, **54–5**
Soyuz 33
space stations **32–5**, 45
Space Launch System (SLS) 44
space stations **32–5**, 45
spacesuits 41
spacewalks 32, 119
spherical nebulas 140
spiral galaxies 98, 99, 118, 144, 145, 146, 147
Milky Way **92–3**
Whirlpool **148–9**
stars
BD+60°2522 127
biggest 6

blue stragglers 133
clusters 107, **132–5**, 134, 136, 137, 148
collisions 111, 133, **150–1**
death of 7
Eta Carinae **108–9**
Flying Saucer 113
formation 7, 93, 108, 114–15, 144, 148, 149
light, time to travel to Earth 99
in the Milky Way 92, 93, 94
neutron stars 122, 133, **150–1**
Pillars of Creation 114–17
protostars 107, 112–13, 116, **124–125, 128–9**
pulsars 122, 123, 150
sun **6–13**, 114
V838 Monocerotis **110–11**
white dwarfs 7, 141, 142
see also nebulas
Stephan, Edouard 144
Stephan's Quintet **144–5**
storms **28–9, 48–9**, 66, 73, 80
Great Dark Spot, Neptune 82, 83
Great Red Spot, Jupiter **68–9**
sulfur 123, 136
sun, Earth's **6–13**
age 114
and auroras 30, 31
eclipses 9
energy 6
gravity 6
and the Milky Way 92
prominences 6
studying **10–11**
sunlight 6, 7, 13, 84
supergiant stars 110, 138
supermassive black holes 92, 118, 144, 145, 147, 148, 153
supernovas 107, 108, 122, 127, 148, 150
and black holes 153
Schwartz, Richard D. 129

T

Tarantula Nebula 106
telescopes
Event Horizon Telescope 153
Herschel's 127
Hubble Space Telescope **118–21**
James Webb Space Telescope 100, **102–5**
tidal tails 144
time, and black holes 153
Titan 76, 77, 78, 79
Tombaugh, Clyde 85
Trapezium Cluster 136, 137
Triton 82, 83

UV

UGC 8335 Galaxy 146
ultraviolet light 13, 41, 108, 113, 116, 127
and telescopes 6, 118, 124
universe **96–153**
age 133

ancient universe 98–9, 119
biggest known star 6
elements of 6
expansion 99, 118
invisible matter 99
strongest magnetic field 150
Uranus **80–1**
UY Scuti 6
V838 Monocerotis **110–11**
Valles Marineris 46, 50
Venera 13, 20
Venus 10, **20–3**
Vesta, asteroid 56, 59
volcanoes 20, 21, 22, 46, 50, 70
cryovolcanoes 57, 76, 84, 85
eruption on Io 91
Voyager 2 82

WXZ

WASP-17b, exoplanet 130
WASP-19b, exoplanet 131
WASP-31b, exoplanet 130
water ice
on dwarf planets 84
on moons 71, 76
on planets 14, 26, 50, 51, 80
water, liquid
on dwarf planets 56, 57
on moons 70, 71, 76
on planets 20, 24, 25, 26, 27, 51, 52
weather, Mars 48
weightlessness 34
white dwarfs 7, 141, 142
winds 48, 68, 82, 83, 131
jet streams 67
stellar 108, 112, 113, 126, 127, 136, 137
Wright Mons 85
x-rays 144, 150
Zarya module, ISS 33
Zeta Orionis 138

Acknowledgments

Smithsonian Enterprises:
Avery Naughton, Licensing Coordinator; Paige Towler,
Editorial Lead; Jill Corcoran, Senior Director, Licensed Publishing; Brigid Ferraro, Vice President of New Business and Licensing; Carol LeBlanc, President

For Smithsonian Astrophysical Observatory:
Drs. Stephanie Jarmak, Scientist; Pepi Fabbiano, Scientist; Rutu Das, Scientist; Scott Wolk, Scientist; Daniel Castro, Scientist; Grant Tremblay, Scientist; and Kimberly Arcand, Scientist

The publisher would like to thank the following for their assistance in the preparation of this book: Steve Hoffman for fact-checking; Jacqui Swan and Claire Watson for design assistance; Stephen Johnson for image resampling; Steve Crozier for picture retouching; Katie John for proofreading; and Carron Brown for the index.

The publisher would like to thank the following for their permission to reproduce their photographs:

(Key: a-above; b-below/bottom; c-center; f-far; l-left; r-right; t-top)

1 NASA: ESA, N. Smith (U. California, Berkeley) et al., and The Hubble Heritage Team (STScI/AURA). **2-3 NASA**: ESA, CSA, STScI. **2 Alamy Stock Photo**: NASA/JPL-Caltech/SwRI/MSSS/Prateek Sarpal/Futuras Fotos (br). **3 ESO**: (bl). **6-7 NASA**: Goddard/SDO. **8-9 Miloslav Druckmüller. 10 NASA**: Johns Hopkins APL/Naval Research Laboratory/Guillermo Stenborg and Brendan Gallagher (clb). **10-11 ESA**: NASA/Johns Hopkins APL/Steve Gribben. **11 NASA**: Johns Hopkins APL/Ben Smith (br). **12-13 Science Photo Library**: NASA'S GODDARD SPACE FLIGHT CENTER SCIENTIFIC VISUALIZATION STUDIO, THE SDO SCIENCE TEAM, AND THE VIRTUAL SOLAR OBSERVATORY. **14 NASA**: Johns Hopkins University Applied Physics Laboratory/Carnegie Institution of Washington (tl). **14-15 NASA**: Johns Hopkins University Applied Physics Laboratory/Carnegie Institution of Washington. **16-17 NASA**: Johns Hopkins University Applied Physics Laboratory/Arizona State University/Carnegie Institution of Washington. Image reproduced courtesy of <i>Science</i>/AAAS.. **18-19 123RF.com**: Natalia Romanova (background). **ESA**: ATG medialab. **Science Photo Library**: European Space Agency/ATG Medialab (b). **18 NASA**: Johns Hopkins University Applied Physics Laboratory/Carnegie Institution of Washington (bl). **19 123RF.com**: Ricard Vaque (www.vaque.com) (br/blackboard). **NASA**: (crb). **20 NASA**: JPL (tl). **20-21 Kevin M. Gill**: (c). **21 ESO**: NASA (br). **22-23 Science Photo Library**: NASA. **24-25 Alamy Stock Photo**: UPI Photo/NASA. **26 Alamy Stock Photo**: Science History Images/Photo Researchers (tc). **naturepl.com**: Tui De Roy (c). **Shutterstock.com**: Alex Brylov (bc); ikumaru (clb). **26-27 Getty Images/iStock**: E+/guenterguni (tc). **Shutterstock.com**: sasha_gerasimov (cb). **27 naturepl.com**: Maxime Aliaga (r). **28-29 NASA**: Goddard MODIS Rapid Response Team. **30-31 Biosphoto**: Christophe Suarez. **31 123RF.com**: swavo (fbr). **NASA**: (bc); JPL/STScI (bl). **Science Photo Library**: NASA/ESA/STSCI (fbl). **Shutterstock.com**: Paniti Alapon (br). **32-33 NASA. 33 Alamy Stock Photo**: NASA (bc). **34-35 ESA**: NASA-S.Cristoforetti/R. Rossi. **36-37 Andrew McCarthy**: (c). **36 Getty Images**: Future/All About Space Magazine/Illustration by Tobias Roetsch (tl). **38-39 Science Photo Library**: Lynette Cook. **40 Alamy Stock Photo**: Dipper Historic (bl). **Dreamstime.com**: Bruno Metal (cla). **NASA**: (br). **Science Photo Library**: Carlos Clarivan (cl, clb). **40-41 NASA. 42-43 ESA**: NASA. **44 Dreamstime.com**: Matthew Trommer/Mtrommer (ftl). **NASA**: Joel Kowsky (tl). **44-45 ESA**: NASA. **45 Alamy Stock Photo**: NASA (cb). Dreamstime.com: Zaur Rahimov (tr). **Science Photo Library**: European Space Agency - D. Ducros (cr). **46-47 ESA**: DLR/FU Berlin/G. Michael. **48-49 NASA**: JPL-Caltech/University of Arizona/NASA Goddard Space Flight Center. **50-51 ESA**: DLR/FU Berlin (G. Neukum) (c). **NASA**: JPL-Caltech/Cornell/ASU (b). **50 Andrea Luck**: creativecommons.org/licenses/by/4.0/deed.en (tl). **51 NASA**: DLR/FU Berlin/Bill Dunford (tl); JPL/Cornell (tr). **Science Photo Library**: NASA/JPL/University Of Arizona (br). **52-53 ESA**: DLR/FU Berlin. **54-55 Dreamstime.com**: Fukume. **55 NASA**: ESA/DLR/FU-Berlin/JPL-Caltech (cb); JPL-Caltech/ASU (tl, br). **56-57 NASA**: JPL-Caltech/UCLA/MPS/DLR/IDA. **57 NASA**: JPL-Caltech/UCLA/MPS/DLR/IDA/PSI (tr). **58 ESO**: JAXA (cra). **Getty Images**: Hulton Archive/NASA/Stringer (tl). **58-59 Getty Images**: NASA/JPL-Caltec/Handout (b). **59 Alamy Stock Photo**: JAXA via AP (br). **NASA**: JPL/USGS (tl, cra). **60 Alamy Stock Photo**: Susan E. Degginger (ftl). **Dreamstime.com**: Adwo (tc). **Shutterstock.com**: Muellek (tl). **60-61 Bridgeman Images**: Christie's Images. **62-63 Science Photo Library**: Herve Conge, ISM. **64-65 123RF.com**: Natalia Romanova. **University of Arizona**: NASA Goddard Space Flight Center (c). **64 NASA**: Goddard/University of Arizona (bl). **65 NASA**: (br); Keegan Barber (cra); Erika Blumenfeld & Joseph Aebersold (cr). **66-67 Alamy Stock Photo**: NASA/JPL-Caltech/SwRI/MSSS/Prateek Sarpal/Futuras Fotos. **67 Getty Images/iStock**: lushik (br). **68-69 Kevin M. Gill. 70 NASA**: JPL/University of Arizona (tl, ca); JPL/DLR (tc). **70-71 NASA**: JPL-Caltech/SwRI/MSSS/Thomas Thomopoulos (bc); JPL/University of Arizona (t). **71 NASA**: JPL-Caltech/SwRI/MSSS/Thomas Thomopoulos (ca); JPL/DLR (bc); JPL/University of Arizona (r). **72-73 NASA**: JPL. **73 NASA**: JPL-Caltech/SSI/Hampton University (tc); JPL-Caltech/Space Science Institute (cr). **74-75 NASA**: JPL-Caltech/SSI. **76 NASA**: JPL/Space Science Institute (cl, cr, bc). **76-77 NASA**: JPL-Caltech/Space Science Institute (bc). **77 Alamy Stock Photo**: NASA Image Collection (br). **NASA**: JPL-Caltech/Space Science Institute (tl, bc); JPL/Space Science Institute (cr); JPL/University of Arizona/University of Idaho (cl). **78-79 123RF.com**: Natalia Romanova. **78 Dreamstime.com**: Alona Stepaniuk (cl). ESA: (bl). 79 ESA: (br). **80-81 NASA**: JPL-Caltech. **81 ESA**: NASA, CSA, STScI (br). **University of Leicester**: (crb). **82-83 NASA**: JPL/Voyager 2. **83 Dreamstime.com**: Wektorygrafika (br). **ESA**: NASA/CSA and STScI (tc). **84-85 Alamy Stock Photo**: NASA/digitaleye/J Marshall - Tribaleye Images. **86 123RF.com**: solarseven (br). **86-87 Science Photo Library**: Rev. Ronald Royer. **87 ESO**: E. Slawik (bl). **Getty Images**: 500px/Jim Miller (br). **88-89 123RF.com**: Natalia Romanova (background). **ESA**: –C. Carreau/ATG medialab. **89 NASA**: Rosetta/Philae/CIVA (br). **90 NASA**: Johns Hopkins University Applied Physics Laboratory/Southwest Research Institute (tl). **90-91 NASA**: Johns Hopkins University Applied Physics Laboratory/Southwest Research Institute. **91 NASA**: Johns Hopkins University Applied Physics Laboratory/Southwest Research Institute (cra, cr, cb). **92 123RF.com**: martiaIred (bl). **Dreamstime.com**: Alexoakenman (clb/rocket); Stockvectorwin (clb). **92-93 NASA**: S. Beckwith (STScI) Hubble Heritage Team, (STScI/AURA), ESA. **94-95 Rachel Roberts. 96 Alamy Stock Photo**: NASA Image Collection (DAPHNIS). **ESA/Hubble**: ESA, the Hubble Heritage Team (STScI/AURA)-ESA/Hubble Collaboration and A. Evans (Univer (ARP 148). **NASA**: JPL-Caltech/SwRI/MSSS/Thomas Thomopoulos (EUROPA); JPL/University of Arizona (IO); JPL/DLR (Callisto, Ganymede); JPL/Space Science Institute (ENCELADUS, DIONE, HYPERION, IAPETUS); JPL/University of Arizona/University of Idaho (TITAN); JPL-Caltech/Space Science Institute (PHOEBE, Pan, MIMAS); ESA, CSA, STScI, Webb ERO Production Team (Tarantula, Cartwheel); ESA, the Hubble Heritage (STScI/AURA)-ESA/Hubble Collaboration, and A. Evans (University of Virginia, Charlottesville/NRAO/Stony Brook University) (ESO 593-8). **97 Alamy Stock Photo**: NASA/digitaleye/J Marshall - Tribaleye Images (Pluto). **ESO**: Event Horizon Telescope Consortium (M87). **98-99 NASA**: ESA, CSA, STScI. **99 123RF.com**: swavo (crb). **Alamy Stock Photo**: Science Photo Library/Mark Garlick (bc). **Dreamstime.com**: DreamStockIcons (crb/Milky way). **100-101 NASA**: ESA, CSA, Leah Hustak (STScI). **102-103 123RF.com**: Natalia Romanova. **102 TurboSquid**: EGPJET3D (tc, tr, br, tl). **103 Dreamstime.com**: Sergey Shvedov (br). **TurboSquid**: EGPJET3D (tl, tc, c, clb). **104-105 NASA**: Desiree Stover. **106 NASA**: ESA, CSA, STScI, Webb ERO Production Team (tl, bl); ESA, CSA, STScI, Klaus Pontoppidan (NASA-JPL), Joel Green (STScI) (br). **106-107 NASA**: ESA, CSA, STScI (t). **107 ESA**: NASA, CSA, STScI, and K. Luhman (Penn State University) and C. Alves de Oliveira (European Space Agency) (tr). **NASA**: ESA, CSA, STScI (tc); ESA, CSA, STScI, Danny Milisavljevic (Purdue University), Ilse De Looze (UGent), Tea Temim (Princeton University) (bl). **108 Alamy Stock Photo**: Science History Images/Photo Researchers (cla). **NASA**: ESA, N. Smith (University of California, Berkeley), and The Hubble Heritage Team (STScI/AURA); (bc); James Gitlin/STScI (clb). **108-109 ESA/Hubble**: NASA, N. Smith (University of Arizona, Tucson), and J. Morse (BoldlyGo Institute, New York). **110-111 ESA/Hubble**: NASA, the Hubble Heritage Team (AURA/STScI). **NASA**: ESA and Z. Levay (STScI) (b). **112-113 ESA**: NASA, CSA, STScI, K. Pontoppidan (STScI), A. Pagan (STScI). **113 Antoine Grelin - www.galactic-hunter.com/**: (bc/Cloud complex). **ESA**: NASA, CSA, STScI, K. Pontoppidan (STScI), A. Pagan (STScI) (bc). **ESO**: NASA/ESA (br); S. Guisard (www.eso.org/~sguisard) (bl). **114-115 ESA**: NASA, CSA, STScI; J. DePasquale, A. Koekemoer, A. Pagan (STScI).. **116-117 ESO. 118 ESA/Hubble**: NASA, Dan Maoz (Tel-Aviv University, Israel, and Columbia University, USA) (tl). 118-119 123RF.com: Natalia Romanova (background). **Dorling Kindersley**: Andy Crawford. **119 ESA/Hubble**: NASA (cr). Getty Images: Pat Gaines (br). **NASA**: ESA, and G. Bacon (STScI) (cra); ESA, H. Teplitz (IPAC, Caltech), M. Rafelski (IPAC, Caltech), Anton M. Koekemoer (STScI), Rogier Windhorst (ASU), Zolt G. Levay (STScI) (crb). **120-121 NASA. 122-123 NASA**: ESA, CSA, STScI, Tea Temim (Princeton University). **122 Alamy Stock Photo**: World History Archive (clb). **NASA**: CXC/HST/ASU/J. Hester et al.; (tc). **124-125 ESA**: Webb, NASA, CSA, T. Ray (Dublin Institute for Advanced Studies). **124 ESA**: Webb, NASA, CSA, T. Ray (Dublin Institute for Advanced Studies) (bl). **126-127 NASA**: ESA, and the Hubble Heritage Team (STScI/AURA). **127 Alamy Stock Photo**: Steven Milne (tc). **128-129 ESA**: NASA, CSA, J. DePasquale (STScI). **129 123RF.com**: swavo (crb). **130 NASA**: ESA (b). **130-131 NASA**: NASA's Goddard Space Flight Center/Francis Reddy (t). **131 NASA:** Ames/SETI Institute/JPL-Caltech (bl); ESA (cr/x2). **132-133 ESA/Hubble**: NASA, R. Cohen. **133 ESO**: (crb). **Science Photo Library**: Mark Garlick (br). **134-135 Dr. Mehmet Hakan ÖZSARA. 136 Alamy Stock Photo**: Science History Images/Photo Researchers (tc); Mark Garlick/Science Photo Library (bl). **Dreamstime.com**: Ljubisa Sujica (clb). **136-137 ESA/Hubble**: NASA, M. Robberto (Space Telescope Science Institute/ESA) and the Hubble Space Telescope Orion Treasury Project Team. **138-139 Alamy Stock Photo**: Ken Crawford/Stocktrek Images. **139 Alamy Stock Photo**: History and Art Collection (crb). **Dreamstime.com**: Alexandr Yurtchenko (bc). **Science Photo Library**: Robert Gendler (br). **140 Alamy Stock Photo**: NG Images (clb/ELLIPTICAL); Science History Images (clb). **ESA/Hubble**: NASA (clb/BIPOLAR). **140-141 NASA**: ESA/Webb, CSA, M. Barlow (UCL), N. Cox (ACRI-ST), R. Wesson (Cardiff University). **142-143 NASA**: ESA, and the Hubble SM4 ERO Team. **142 ESA/Hubble**: NASA (clb). **NASA**: H.E. Bond and E. Nelan (Space Telescope Science Institute, Baltimore, Md.); M. Barstow and M. Burleigh (University of Leicester, U.K.); and J.B. Holberg (University of Arizona) (br). **144-145 NASA**: ESA, CSA, STScI. **144 NASA**: CXC/SAO; IR (Spitzer)/JPL-Caltech; IR (Webb)/ESA/CSA/STScI (tc). **Shutterstock.com**: Cinefootage Visuals (cl); Yavier Mendoza (clb). **146 ESA/Hubble**: NASA, the Hubble Heritage Team (STScI/AURA)-ESA/Hubble Collaboration and A. Evans (University of Virginia, Charlottesville/NRAO/Stony Brook University) (cra); NASA, ESA, the Hubble Heritage Team (STScI/AURA)-ESA/Hubble Collaboration and A. Evans (University of Virginia, Charlottesville/NRAO/Stony Brook University) (bl). **NASA**: ESA, the Hubble Heritage (STScI/AURA)-ESA/Hubble Collaboration, and A. Evans (University of Virginia, Charlottesville/NRAO/Stony Brook University) (tl). **147 ESA/Hubble**: ESA, the Hubble Heritage Team (STScI/AURA)-ESA/Hubble Collaboration and A. Evans (Univer (br). **NASA**: ESA, the Hubble Heritage (STScI/AURA)-ESA/Hubble Collaboration, and A. Evans (University of Virginia, Charlottesville/NRAO/Stony Brook University) (tl); ESA, the Hubble Heritage (STScI/AURA)-ESA/Hubble Collaboration, and K. Noll (STScI) (tr); ESA, and Z. Levay (STScI) (bl). **148-149 NASA**: ESA, S. Beckwith (STScI), and The Hubble Heritage Team (STScI/AURA). **148 NASA**: Robert P. Kirshner/Harvard-Smithsonian Center for Astrophysics, (br). **149 123RF.com**: swavo (crb). **150 Dreamstime.com**: Archangel80889 (cb/cloud). **Getty Images/iStock**: rvika (bc). **Max Planck Institute of Radioastronomy**: Mark Myers/OzGrav-Swinburne, licence CC BY-NC-ND, Created with UniverseSandbox (cl). **Shutterstock.com**: Gilbert - Illustration (cb). **151 Carnegie Institution for Science**: Robin Dienel/Carnegie Science. **152 ESO**: Event Horizon Telescope Consortium (br, bc). **152-153 Science Photo Library**: Alfred Pasieka. **153 ESO**: Event Horizon Telescope Consortium (tr). **Science Photo Library**: Mark Garlick (bc)

Cover images: *Front:* **ESA/Hubble**: NASA, N. Smith (University of Arizona, Tucson), and J. Morse (BoldlyGo Institute, New York) bc; **NASA**: ESA, Massimo Robberto (STScI, ESA), Hubble Space Telescope Orion Treasury Project Team tl, ESA, N. Smith (U. California, Berkeley) et al., and The Hubble Heritage Team (STScI/AURA) bl; **Dr. Mehmet Hakan ÖZSARA**: c; **Shutterstock.com**: Dima Zel tr; *Back:* **123RF.com**: Natalia Romanova cr/(background), bl/ (background); **Alamy Stock Photo**: Steven Milne bc, NASA/JPL-Caltech/SwRI/MSSS/Prateek Sarpal/Futuras Fotos cl; **Dorling Kindersley**: Andy Crawford cr; **ESO**: tc; **NASA**: Johns Hopkins University Applied Physics Laboratory/Arizona State University/Carnegie Institution of Washington. Image reproduced courtesy of <i>Science</i>/AAAS. cra, JPL/Space Science Institute tl